M
O
N
D
O

C
A
N
I
N
E

ALSO BY

JON WINOKUR

Writers on Writing
The Portable Curmudgeon
Zen to Go
A Curmudgeon's Garden of Love
Friendly Advice

A DUTTON BOOK

MONDO CANINE

COMPILED AND EDITED BY
JON WINOKUR

DUTTON
Published by the Penguin Group
Penguin Books USA Inc., 375 Hudson Street,
New York, New York 10014, U.S.A.
Penguin Books Ltd, 27 Wrights Lane, London W8 5TZ, England
Penguin Books Australia Ltd, Ringwood, Victoria, Australia
Penguin Books Canada Ltd, 10 Alcorn Avenue,
Toronto, Ontario, Canada M4V 3B2
Penguin Books (N.Z.) Ltd, 182–190 Wairau Road,
Auckland 10, New Zealand

Penguin Books Ltd, Registered Offices:
Harmondsworth, Middlesex, England

First published by Dutton, an imprint of New American Library, a
division of Penguin Books USA Inc.
Distributed in Canada by McClelland & Stewart Inc.

First Printing, October, 1991
1 3 5 7 9 10 8 6 4 2

 REGISTERED TRADEMARK—MARCA REGISTRADA

Library of Congress Cataloging-in-Publication Data
Mondo canine / compiled and edited by Jon Winokur.
p.   cm.
Includes indexes.
ISBN 0-525-93352-2
1. Dogs—Quotations, maxims, etc.   2. Dogs—Humor.   I. Winokur, Jon.
PN6084.D64M6   1991
636.7′0207—dc20   91-2607
CIP

Printed in the United States of America
Set in Spartan & Bodoni Book
Designed by Michael Ian Kaye
Picture research by Gillian Speeth

TO PEPPIE,

BEST·OF·BREED

ACKNOWLEDGMENTS

Thanks for everything: Bess & Stella, Betsy, Billie, Bon-Bon, Boy, Buddy, Casey, Fritz, Garbo, Gina, Ginger, Hans, Jeff, Lord Baltimore, Maggie, Mugsy, Maxie/Pierre, Muffin, Nicky, Noodles, Pacer, Pepper, Petey, Poco, Porky, Ranger, Rufus, Sam, Spot, Suki & Biscuit, Sweeper, Toots, and Tuffy. And thanks to Jim Auckland, Berton Averre, Roger Beerworth, Peter Bell, Jennifer Bassing, Tony Bill, Philip Blank, Reid and Karen Boates, Margie Carlin, Roger Caras, Susan Christian, C. E. Crimmins, Norrie Epstein, Nancy Hathaway, Vicki Hearne, Stephen Hulburt, H. Myles Jacob, Michael Jamison, Leo Jarzomb, Margo Kaufman, Michael Ian Kaye, Merle Kessler, Rachel Klayman, Irv Lander, Howard LeNoble, David Levitas, Constance Lofton, Gary Luke, Bonnie Mader, Rick Miglia, Susan Nethery, Howard Ogden, Kristin Olson, Paul Ossmann, Glenn Parsons, Laurie Pearlstein, Lee Perry, Al and Betty Rasof, Steve Schuhle, Amy Shapira, Toby Schmidt, Nola Shrewsberry, Judy Sims, Beth Siniawsky, Chandra and Chris and Gillian Speeth, Nancy and Jim Steele, Neil Stuart, Linda Takahashi, Pam and Tracy Thomas, Rosemary A. Thurber, Roberta Vesley, LuAnn Walther, William K. West, Mark Wolgin, Penny Work and Steve Zorn. I am especially grateful to Elinor Winokur, without whom this book (and I) would not exist.

C O N T E N T S

INTRODUCTION

If dogs didn't exist, we'd have to invent them. They are clean, cheerful, brave, and faithful. They consistently display the best qualities of humans and few, if any, of the bad ones ("All the virtues of man, without his vices," in Byron's phrase). They are the only species in the animal kingdom to have truly embraced human beings, and when it comes to friendship, they put us to shame. They give unconditional love and undying loyalty in return for regular meals and an occasional pat on the head.

We are literally and legally their masters, with absolute power of life and death over them. We are their reason for being: after a thousand generations of controlled breeding, puppies are born genetically programmed to please humans, and they grow up to be devoted friends whose goodwill enriches our lives. And many of us seem to have a built-in attraction to dogs: after a thousand generations of living with them, perhaps we've evolved *dogness* receptors in our brains.

The relationship between dogs and humans is the oldest, most durable, and most complex alliance between two species in history. The wolves from which dogs evolved were probably domesticated during the Stone Age, but precisely what first brought

Man and Dog together is not known. It may have been their complementary hunting skills. With all his technology, his spears, traps, and snares, Man the Hunter had one severe handicap: his nose was woefully inadequate. Wolves, on the other hand, had superb scenting abilities, and they lived and hunted in packs under the command of a single individual, so it would not have been difficult for them to accept a human as their "pack leader." Or perhaps, when ten or twenty thousand years ago wolves started hanging around campfires for handouts, their value as sentinels became apparent, cavemen encouraged them with occasional scraps, and the symbiotic relationship developed from there. Or maybe prehistoric man hunted wolves, adopted the orphaned pups as a walking food supply, and some of the pups inevitably survived as pets.

These are plausible theories, and the truth may be a combination of them all, but I suspect another reason for the unique bond: have you ever seen a dog struggling to scratch itself on a stationary object? What a pleasure the clawing, tickling, massaging human hand must give them. Dogs love to be petted, and human hands are perfect petting devices. Thus the same physical equipment that gave humans dominance over all the other species—the club-wielding, rock-throwing, fire-starting, tool-making *hand*—has given us gentle mastery over dogs.

Dogs and people have other traits in common. Like humans, male and female wolves mate and live in more or less monogamous couples; modern men and dogs live together in dwellings natural to them both (dogs may regard a house, with its various rooms, as a multichambered den); unlike most other animals, which cast off childish things upon reaching physical and psychological maturity, both humans and dogs love to *play* well into adulthood; and individuals from both species occasionally display evidence of having a conscience.

Aside from these common characteristics, on our part we have done little to accommodate dogs. But with the exception of a few petty examples of unseemly behavior involving urination, defecation, and indiscreet sniffing and licking, on their part they have learned our peculiarities and adapted to them readily. Their keen senses enable them to *read* us—the average dog has a vocabulary of several dozen words and can interpret human facial expressions and body language with remarkable accuracy. They have an intense affinity for humans, commiserating when we're sad and sharing our joy when we're happy. And it is increasingly apparent that just having them around makes us healthier: studies have shown that their presence reduces stress and lowers blood pressure, and that heart patients tend to live longer if there's a dog in the house. Which suggests what may be their greatest contribution: dogs *humanize* an environment.

All this and they earn their keep too: dogs have been eager accomplices in all manner of human endeavor from war to frisbee. They serve as eyes for the blind and ears for the deaf, as therapists and rescuers, as detectives and beasts of burden. *Canis familiaris* is, after all, a custom species: we have bred dogs into a wide variety of shapes and sizes the better to hunt, tend our livestock, defend our homes, or just sit in our laps.

Unfortunately, we do not always return their devotion. We confine them for long periods in basements and garages, in parked cars, in the cargo holds of jetliners, in metal cages euphemistically called "kennels." We chain them up in spaces we call "yards" and "runs." We breed them into grotesque mutations, systematically mutilating them in the process (we "crop" their ears, "dock" their tails, and even surgically "debark" them). We exploit them cruelly for our amusement: organized dog fights were common until the turn of this century and still go on in some parts of the United States. We surrender them by the thousands each year to animal "shelters" where most of them are eventually "destroyed," and we use them in medical research despite mounting evidence that their sacrifice contributes little to the advancement of science. We poison them, shoot them, trap them, and, in some parts of the world, we butcher and eat them. In China and Korea to this day puppies are fattened and slaughtered before they're a year old. We impute human values to them that they don't possess and then punish them for not living up to our expectations. We betray their trust, and thereby fail to be worthy of it.

But fortunately, some of us do reciprocate their ardor. Some of us are *fans*. I myself find dogs irresistible. Can't take my eyes off them. (Why are movie dogs notorious "scene stealers"? Because they're the most appealing thing on the screen.) When I'm driving along and I see a proud terrier trotting along the sidewalk or a blithesome retriever in the back of a pickup, I'll ignore the traffic and follow him in my rearview mirror until long after I've passed him.

What's the attraction? Maybe it's that dogs have a spontaneity we lost long ago. They are our "gods of frolic." They're . . . *characters* with distinct . . . *personalities.* There are earnest dogs, sneaky dogs, taciturn dogs, "hyper" dogs, shy dogs, motherly dogs, even neurotic dogs who exhibit what in humans is termed "obsessive compulsive behavior." Hence the otherwise equable Boston terrier who assaults the vacuum cleaner whenever it is taken from the closet; the poodle who attacks the mail as it comes through the slot; the dog who chews bowling balls; another who endlessly pushes a large rock to-and-fro in the backyard; and the small, moplike terrier who latches onto a sock with its teeth and holds on for dear life while its master swabs the floor with it.

For a long time I have worshiped dogs from afar, observing them with increasing fascination. For example, I had long considered the idea that dogs "smile" a gross anthropomorphism, and when I began the research for this book, I set out to expose it as wishful thinking. But to my astonishment, every one of the experts I consulted believes that dogs do indeed smile, and I found repeated references to "smiling," "grinning," and "laughing" dogs in novels and short stories. *Why* do they smile? It's clearly not in the repertoire of natural canine expressions. The best explanation is that dogs have learned to mimic the human smile as an expression of joy the better to communicate with us on our own terms. Typical.

This book is a celebration of the canine spirit, an exploration of the joys of *Hundkeit,* an unabashed paean to those gentle, generous, genuine creatures, those virtuosi of *joie de vivre,* whose friendship ennobles us.

■ J.W.
PACIFIC PALISADES, CALIFORNIA
DECEMBER 1990

M
O
N
D
O

C
A
N
I
N
E

H U N D K E I T

The dog is man's best friend.
He has a tail on one end.
Up in front he has teeth
And four legs underneath.

■ OGDEN NASH,
"AN INTRODUCTION TO DOGS"

It has been twenty thousand years since man and dog formed their partnership. That we have altered the dog genetically is well understood; it is hardly known how they changed us. Since dogs could hear and smell better than men, we could concentrate on sight. Since courage is commonplace in dogs, men's adrenal glands could shrink. Dogs, by making us more efficient predators, gave us time to think. In short, dogs civilized us.

■ DONALD McCAIG,
EMINENT DOGS, DANGEROUS MEN

The dog is mentioned in the Bible eighteen times—the cat not even once.

■ W.E. FARBSTEIN

Take a dog for a companion and a stick in your hand.

■ ENGLISH PROVERB

Two dogs will kill a lion.

■ HEBREW PROVERB

Money will buy a pretty good dog, but it won't buy the wag of his tail.

■ JOSH BILLINGS

MONDO
CANINE

Say something idiotic and nobody but a dog politely wags his tail.
∎ VIRGINIA GRAHAM

The dog was created especially for children. He is the god of frolic.
∎ HENRY WARD BEECHER

The greatest pleasure of a dog is that you may make a fool of yourself with him, and not only will he not scold you, but he will make a fool of himself too.
∎ SAMUEL BUTLER

Histories are more full of examples of the fidelity of dogs than of friends.
∎ ALEXANDER POPE

No man can be condemned for owning a dog. As long as he has a dog he has a friend, and the poorer he gets, the better friend he has.
∎ WILL ROGERS

The average dog is a nicer person than the average person.
∎ ANDY ROONEY

A dog is the only thing on this earth that loves you more than he loves himself.
∎ JOSH BILLINGS

To err is human, to forgive canine.
∎ ANONYMOUS

There is no doubt that every healthy, normal boy (if there is such a thing in these days of Child Study) should own a dog at some time in his life, preferably between the ages of forty-five and fifty.
∎ ROBERT BENCHLEY

MONDO CANINE

They are superior to human beings as companions. They do not quarrel or argue with you. They never talk about themselves but listen to you while you talk about yourself, and keep up an appearance of being interested in the conversation.
■ JEROME K. JEROME

To his dog, every man is Napoleon, hence the popularity of dogs.
■ ALDOUS HUXLEY

3

Maybe he figured it all out and decided that a licking now and again and no work was a whole lot better than work all the time and no licking. He was intelligent enough for such a computation. I tell you, I've sat and looked into that dog's eyes till the shivers ran up and down my spine and the marrow crawled like yeast, what of the intelligence I saw shining out. I can't express myself about that intelligence. It is beyond mere words. I saw it, that's all. At times it was like gazing into a human soul, to look into his eyes; and what I saw there frightened me and started all sorts of ideas in my own mind of reincarnation and all the rest. I tell you I sensed something big in that brute's eyes; there was a message there, but I wasn't big enough myself to catch it. Whatever it was (I know I'm making a fool of myself)—whatever it was, it baffled me. I can't give an inkling of what I saw in that brute's eyes; it wasn't light, it wasn't color; it was something that moved, away back, when the eyes themselves weren't moving. And I guess I didn't see it move, either; I only sensed that it moved. It was an expression, that's what it was, and I got an impression of it. No, it was different from a mere expression; it was more than that. I don't know what it was, but it gave me a feeling of kinship just the same. Oh, no, not sentimental kinship. It was, rather, a kinship of equality. Those eyes never pleaded like a deer's eyes. They challenged. No, it wasn't defiance. It was just a calm assumption of equality. And I don't think it was deliberate. My belief is that it was unconscious on his part. It was there because it was there, and it couldn't help shining out. No, I don't mean shine. It didn't shine; it *moved*. I know I'm talking rot, but if you'd looked into that animal's eyes the way I have, you'd understand.

■ JACK LONDON,
"THAT SPOT"

I've seen a look in dogs' eyes, a quickly vanishing look of amazed contempt, and I am convinced that dogs think humans are nuts.

■ JOHN STEINBECK,
TRAVELS WITH CHARLEY

From the dog's point of view, his master is an elongated and abnormally cunning dog.   ■ MABEL LOUISE ROBINSON

Ever consider what they must think of us? I mean, here we come back from a grocery store with the most amazing haul—chicken, pork, half a cow. . . . They must think we're the greatest hunters on earth!
■ ANNE TYLER

Dogs, the foremost snobs in creation, are quick to note the difference between a well-clad and a disreputable stranger.
■ ALBERT PAYSON TERHUNE,
THE COMING OF LAD

We are alone, absolutely alone on this chance planet; and amid all the forms of life that surround us, not one, excepting the dog, has made an alliance with us.   ■ MAURICE MAETERLINCK,
"OUR FRIEND, THE DOG"

5

The small percentage of dogs that bite people is monumental proof that the dog is the most benign, forgiving creature on earth.
■ W.R. KOEHLER,
THE KOEHLER METHOD OF DOG TRAINING

If you pick up a starving dog and make him prosperous, he will not bite you. This is the principal difference between a dog and a man.
■ MARK TWAIN

Barking dogs don't bite, but they themselves don't know it.
■ SHOLEM ALEICHEM

Living with a dog is easy—like living with an idealist.
■ H.L. MENCKEN

You think dogs will not be in heaven? I tell you, they will be there long before any of us. ■ ROBERT LOUIS STEVENSON

Dogs are expert at inflicting remorse.
■ J.R. ACKERLEY,
MY DOG TULIP

FOOVIEW (foo' view) n. The ability of a dog to inflict guilt from any angle in the room while he watches his master eat.
■ RICH HALL,
SNIGLETS

(c) Elliott Erwitt/Magnum Photos

I don't eat anything that a dog won't eat. Like sushi. Ever see a dog eat sushi? He just sniffs it and says, "I don't think so." And this is an animal that licks between its legs and sniffs fire hydrants.
■ BILLIAM CORONEL

MONDO CANINE

If dogs could talk, perhaps we could find it as hard to get along with them as we do with people.

■ KAREL CAPEK

If dogs could talk it would take a lot of the fun out of owning one.

■ ANDY ROONEY

So many get reformed through religion. I got reformed through dogs. I underwent menopause without taking even an aspirin, because I was so busy whelping puppies. Dogs saved my life. I recommend having four-legged animals to cure the mid-life crisis.

■ LINA BASQUETTE

It is a strange thing, love. Nothing but love has made the dog lose his wild freedom, to become the servant of man. And this very servility or completeness of love makes him a term of deepest contempt—"You dog!"

■ D.H. LAWRENCE, "REX"

The best way to get a puppy is to beg for a baby brother—and they'll settle for a puppy every time.

■ WINSTON PENDELTON

I love a dog. He does nothing for political reasons.

■ WILL ROGERS

My public loves dogs. One pitch with a hound is worth ten thousand words.

■ ANDY GRIFFITH IN
A FACE IN THE CROWD
(SCREENPLAY BY BUDD SCHULBERG)

All knowledge, the totality of all questions and all answers, is contained in the dog.

■ FRANZ KAFKA,
"INVESTIGATIONS OF A DOG"

When thinking of him, what a crowd of memories come back, bringing with them the perfume of fallen days! What delights and glamour, what long hours of effort, discouragements, and secret fears did he not watch over; how many thousand walks did we not go on together, so that we still turn to see if he is following at his padding gait, attentive to the invisible trails. Not the least hard thing to bear when they go from us, these quiet friends, is that they carry away with them so many years of our own lives. Yet, if they find warmth therein, who would grudge them those years that they have so guarded? Nothing else of us can they take to lie upon with outstretched paws and chin stretched to the ground; and, whatever they take, be sure they have deserved.

■ JOHN GALSWORTHY,
"MEMORIES"

Dogs' lives are too short. Their only fault, really.

■ AGNES SLIGH TURNBULL

A dog can't get struck by lightning. You know why? 'Cause he's too close to the ground. See, lightning strikes tall things. Now, if they were giraffes out there in that field, now then we'd be in trouble. But you sure don't have to worry about dogs.

■ DON KNOTTS ON
"THE ANDY GRIFFITH SHOW"

Dog! At the price of the repose which is dear to your heart, you came to me when I was dismayed and brought low. You did not laugh, as any young person of my own species would have done. It is true that however joyous or terrible nature may appear to you at times, she never inspires you with a sense of the ridiculous. And it is for that very reason that you are the surest friend a man can have.

■ ANATOLE FRANCE,
"THE COMING OF RIQUET"

No one appreciates the very special genius of your conversation as a dog does. ■ CHRISTOPHER MORLEY

I would rather see the portrait of a dog that I know, than all the allegorical paintings they can show me in the world.

■ SAMUEL JOHNSON

There is no faith which has never yet been broken except that of a truly faithful dog. ■ KONRAD LORENZ,
KING SOLOMON'S RING

Those sighs of a dog! They go to the heart so much more deeply than the sighs of our own kind because they are utterly unintended, regardless of effect, emerging from one who, heaving them, knows not that they have escaped him! ■ JOHN GALSWORTHY

With the exception of women, there is nothing on earth so agreeable or necessary to the comfort of man as the dog.

■ EDWARD JESSE,
ANECDOTE OF DOGS

There are three faithful friends—an old wife, an old dog, and ready money. ■ BENJAMIN FRANKLIN,
POOR RICHARD'S ALMANACK

To a man the greatest blessing is individual liberty; to a dog it is the last word in despair. ■ WILLIAM LYON PHELPS

MONDO CANINE

If you eliminate smoking and gambling, you will be amazed to find that almost all an Englishman's pleasures can be, and mostly are, shared by his dog. ■ GEORGE BERNARD SHAW

I think we are drawn to dogs because they are the uninhibited creatures we might be if we weren't certain we knew better. They fight for honor at the first challenge, make love with no moral restraint, and they do not for all their marvelous instincts appear to know about death. Being such wonderfully uncomplicated beings, they need us to do their worrying. ■ GEORGE BIRD EVANS,
"TROUBLES WITH BIRD DOGS"

I always like a dog so long as he isn't spelled backward. ■ G.K. CHESTERTON

I never yet knew a dog that had sense enough to unwind his own chain when he had tangled it around a tree, or gotten it snarled in the brambles. I never knew a dog with the simple brainpower to lay a stick on a hearth-fire when the blaze flickered low—although such a dog loved the fire and had seen it replenished in that way a thousand times. I never knew a dog with sense enough to cease worshiping a human fool. ■ ALBERT PAYSON TERHUNE

Nobody can fully understand the meaning of love unless he's owned a dog. He can show you more honest affection with a flick of his tail than a man can gather through a lifetime of handshakes. I can't think of anything that brings me closer to tears than when my old dog—completely exhausted after a full and hard day in the field—limps away from her nice spot in front of the fire and comes over to where I'm sitting and puts her head in my lap, a paw over my knee and closes

MONDO CANINE

her eyes and goes back to sleep. I don't know what I've done to deserve that kind of friend.
■ GENE HILL,
"THE DOG MAN"

Most dogs are earnest, which is why most people like them. You can say any fool thing to a dog, and the dog will give you this look that says, "My God, you're RIGHT! I NEVER would have thought of that!" So we come to think of dogs as being understanding and loving and compassionate, and after a while we hardly even notice that they spend the bulk of their free time circling around with other dogs to see which one can sniff the other the most times in the crotch.
■ DAVE BARRY,
"EARNING A COLLIE DEGREE"

Dogs love company. They place it first in their short list of needs.
■ J.R. ACKERLEY,
MY DOG TULIP

Dogs love laughter, clapping and jokes. I had a little dog who laughed when we laughed although she hadn't the slightest idea what she was laughing about. It was the happiness that pervaded the room when we were laughing that entered her brain and made her feel happy so she laughed too.
■ BARBARA WOODHOUSE,
NO BAD DOGS

When a dog wants to hang out the "Do Not Disturb" sign, as all of us do now and then, he is regarded as a traitor to his species.
■ RAMONA C. ALBERT

The Egyptians named the brightest star in the heavens the dog star, Sirius. Well-placed Romans kept a dog in the atrium and set in the

11

walls of their dwellings a mosaic or drawing calling attention to the watchdog's fidelity in the words *cave canem*—"beware of the dog." A legal doctrine even developed in English jurisprudence to the effect that a dog's character was presumed to be good until the contrary was shown. ■ GERALD CARSON

(c) Neil Hoyte, c/o Portfolio Gallery, London

12

The place of dogs in mythology . . . appears to be universal. Greco-Roman literature features dogs in various roles. Think of Hecate's hounds, the hunting dogs of Diana, and Cerberus of Hades. Then there is Asclepius, god of medicine, who as an infant was saved by being suckled by a bitch. And of course, Romulus and Remus (to stretch a point). Egypt had her share of dogs in mythology, which appear prominently in wall painting, and may have come to us intact as mummies.

Persian mythology features a dog in the account of creation. The Aztec and Maya civilizations include one as well. Various tribes of

Africa, the Maoris of New Zealand and other Polynesian cultures, along with the venerable traditions of the Hindu and Buddhist have all found some place for a dog in the legends that have been handed down in both oral and literary traditions.

■ THE MONKS OF NEW SKETE,
HOW TO BE YOUR DOG'S BEST FRIEND

There's facts about dogs, and there's opinions about them. The dogs have the facts, and the humans have the opinions. If you want facts about a dog, always get them straight from the dog. If you want opinions, get them from humans.

■ MOJAVE DAN IN
KINSHIP WITH ALL LIFE
BY J. ALLEN BOONE

You never know what goes on in a dog's head. He will do a thing, and there are various ways to explain it. The best way usually is the simple and instinctive way, but I am not sure it is always right. In the end there is really no way to tell. ■ DION HENDERSON,
"BROKEN TREATY"

13

Dogs aren't born knowing what or what not to do; they only learn like children. Having once been punished, dogs remember, but like children, they hope they won't be caught in the act. Dogs can be so conscience-stricken that I have seen an innocent one creep and crawl away in shame when another dog has committed the crime, and the innocent dog has been punished in error. ■ BARBARA WOODHOUSE,
NO BAD DOGS

Every human child must learn the universe fresh. Every stockdog pup carries the universe within him. Humans have externalized their wisdom—stored it in museums, libraries, the expertise of the learned. Dog wisdom is inside the blood and bones. Humans trace their ancestors through books and records. Nop's ancestors were what he knew.

■ DONALD McCAIG,
NOP'S TRIALS

Dogs' noses are to ours as a map of the surface of our brains is to a map of the surface of an egg. A dog who did comparative psychology might easily worry about our consciousness or lack thereof, the way we worry about the consciousness of a squid.

■ VICKI HEARNE,
ADAM'S TASK

The bitch alternately sniffed at the surfaces popular in canine society and made its own contribution to The Dog's World, that archetype of the wall newspaper.　　　　■ A. CALDER-MARSHALL,
THE MAGIC OF MY YOUTH

We see . . . how he is at once in a world of smells of which we know nothing, which so occupy and absorb his attention as to make him practically blind to everything about him and deaf to all sounds, even to his master's voice impatiently calling him.

■ W.H. HUDSON,
A HIND IN RICHMOND PARK

I produced another bottle of sodium iodide and repeated the injection with Judy's nose again almost touching the needle as she sniffed avidly. Her eyes were focused on the injection site with fierce concentration and so intent was she on extracting the full savour that she occasionally blew out her nostrils with a sharp blast before recommencing her inspection.　　　　■ JAMES HERRIOT,
"JUDY THE NURSE DOG"

MONDO CANINE

The canine mind is quite capable of disapproval. I took my own dog almost everywhere with me but if I left him at home . . . he would lie under our bed, sulking, and when he emerged, would studiously ignore us for an hour or two. ■ JAMES HERRIOT,
"MYRTLE"

The dog has seldom been successful in pulling man up to its level of sagacity, but man has frequently dragged the dog down to his.
■ JAMES THURBER

Now that we are re-established here [in Italy], we haven't another dog; dogs aren't so necessary to one as they seem to be in England, and they have an odd and tactless way of making one feel that one *is* in England—perhaps because they don't gesticulate and don't speak one word of Italian and seem to expect to find rabbits among the olive-groves and to have bones of Welsh mutton thrown to them from the luncheon table. ■ MAX BEERBOHM,
LETTERS OF MAX BEERBOHM 1892-1956

Dogs are the most wonderful creatures to own because they don't brood about the past, they don't hold a grudge against their owners, they seem to know when correction is fair and just, and they definitely have consciences, which to me proves they also have souls, although I am told this is not possible and in the next world we shall not see our dogs again! ■ BARBARA WOODHOUSE,
NO BAD DOGS

Show dogs have been bred to live off the fat of the land. The only feathers they've ever seen were on the hat of some female judge.
■ RICHARD A. WOLTERS,
GUN DOG

Show dogs and their handlers remind me of Brooke Shields and her mother: an incredibly disheveled person tethered to an impeccably groomed animal. ■ MARGO KAUFMAN

A yard dog is the best dog to have. Yard dogs spend their days under trucks to stay out of the hot sun, and they are recognizable by the oil and grease on their backs and by the humble way they walk sideways toward the individual calling them.

■ LEWIS GRIZZARD

David Hare told me a merry Bond story today. Edward was at the Vienna Burgtheater surrounded by earnest, sweating technicians giving their all. A dog got into the auditorium and scampered about. Edward said in a loud voice, "Thank goodness for something human."

■ PETER HALL,
PETER HALL'S DIARIES

Dogs are very different from cats in that they can be images of human virtue. They are like us. ■ IRIS MURDOCH

Just as [the train] was starting there shot in a liver-colored dog, followed by three middle-aged and important-looking gentlemen. The dog, a Chow, took the seat opposite to me. He had a quiet dignity about him. He struck me as more Chinese than dog.

■ JEROME K. JEROME,
MY LIFE AND TIMES

I once saw an Alsatian give himself a cooling drink of water from a tap set in the wall near the quayside at Weymouth. By standing on his hind legs and steadying himself with one paw on the wall he was able to press down on the top of the tap with the other paw, thereby turning it on.   ■ J.G. REES

A dog is not "almost human" and I know of no greater insult to the canine race than to describe it as such. The dog can do many things which man cannot do, never could do and never will do.

■ JOHN HOLMES

(c) Antonio Mendoza: *Untitled*, from the Leela Series, 1979, courtesy of the Witkin Gallery, Inc., New York

Dogs are not people dressed up in fur coats, and to deny them their nature is to do them great harm.

■ JEANNE SCHINTO,
THE LITERARY DOG

All in the town were still asleep
When the sun came up with a shout
and a leap.
In the lonely streets, unseen by man,
A little dog danced
And the day began.

■ RUPERT BROOKE

Imagine you are dead. After many years in exile, you are permitted to cast a single glance earthward. You see a lamppost and an old dog lifting its leg against it. You are so moved that you cannot help sobbing.

■ PAUL KLEE

19

MONDO
CANINE

A PREFACE TO DOGS

JAMES THURBER

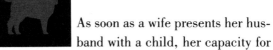

As soon as a wife presents her husband with a child, her capacity for worry becomes acuter: she hears more burglars, she smells more things burning, she begins to wonder, at the theater or the dance, whether her husband left his service revolver in the nursery. This goes on for years and years. As the child grows older, the mother's original major fear—that the child was exchanged for some other infant at the hospital—gives way to even more magnificent doubts and suspicions: she suspects that the child is not bright, she doubts that it will be happy, she is sure that it will become mixed up with the wrong sort of people.

This insistence of parents on dedicating their lives to their children is carried on year after year in the face of all that dogs have done, and are doing, to prove how much happier the parent-child relationship can become, if managed without sentiment, worry, or dedication. Of course, the theory that dogs have a saner family life than humans is an old one, and it was in order to ascertain whether the notion is pure legend or whether it is based on observable fact that I have for many years made a careful study of the family life of dogs. My conclusions entirely support the theory that dogs have a saner family life than people.

In the first place, the husband leaves on a woodchuck-hunting expedition just as soon as he can, which is very soon, and never comes back. He doesn't write, makes no provision for the care or maintenance of his family, and is not liable to prosecution because he doesn't. The wife doesn't care where he is, never wonders if he is thinking about her, and although she may start at the slightest footstep, doesn't do so because she is hoping against hope that it is Spot. No lady dog has ever been known to set her friends against her husband or put detectives on his trail.

This same lack of sentimentality is carried out in the mother dog's relationship to her young. For six weeks—but only six weeks—she looks after them religiously, feeds them (they come clothed), washes their ears, fights off cats, old women, and wasps that come nosing around, makes the bed, and rescues the puppies when they crawl under the floorboards of the barn or get lost in an old boot. She does all these things, however, without fuss, without that loud and elaborate show of solicitude and alarm which a woman displays in rendering some exaggerated service to her child.

At the end of six weeks, the mother dog ceases to lie awake at night harking for ominous sounds; the next morning she snarls at the puppies after breakfast and routs them all out of the house. "This is forever," she informs them, succinctly. "I have my own life to live, automobiles to chase, grocery boys' shoes to snap at, rabbits to pursue. I can't be washing and feeding a lot of big six-week-old dogs any longer. That phase is definitely over." The family life is thus terminated, and the mother dismisses the children from her mind—frequently as many as eleven at one time—as easily as she did her husband. She is now free to devote herself to her career and to the novel and astonishing things of life.

In the case of one family of dogs that I observed, the mother, a large black dog with long ears and a keen zest for living, tempered only by an immoderate fear of toads and turtles, kicked ten puppies out of the house at the end of six weeks to the day—it was a Monday. Fortunately for my observations, the puppies had no place to go, since they hadn't made any plans, and so they just hung around the barn, now and again trying to patch things up with their mother. She refused, however, to entertain any proposition leading to a resumption of home life, pointing out firmly that she was, by inclination, a chaser of bicycles and a hearth-fire-watcher, both of which activities would be insupportably cluttered up by the presence of ten helpers. The bicycle-chasing field was overcrowded, anyway, she explained, and the hearth-fire-watching field even more so. "We could chase parades together," suggested one of the dogs, but she refused to be touched, snarled, and drove him off.

It is only for a few weeks that the cast-off puppies make overtures to their mother in regard to the reestablishment of a home. At the end of that time, by some natural miracle that I am unable clearly to understand, the puppies suddenly one day don't recognize their mother any more, and she doesn't recognize them. It is as if they had never met, and is a fine idea, giving both parties a clean break and a chance for a fresh start. Once, some months after this particular family had broken up, and the pups had been sold, one of them, named Liza, was brought back to "the old nest" for a visit. The mother dog of course didn't recognize the puppy and promptly bit her in the hip. They were separated, each grumbling something about you never know what kind of dogs you're going to meet. Here was no silly affecting reunion, no sentimental tears, no bitter intimations of neglect or forgetfulness or desertion.

If a pup is not sold or given away, but is brought up in the same household with its mother, the two will fight bitterly, sometimes twenty or thirty times a day, for maybe a month. This is very trying to whoever owns the dogs, particularly if they are sentimentalists who grieve because mother and child don't know each other. The condition finally clears up: the two dogs grow to tolerate each other and, beyond growling a little under their breath about how it takes all kinds of dogs to make up a world, get along fairly well together when their paths cross. I know of one mother dog and her half-grown daughter who sometimes spend the whole day together hunting woodchucks, although they don't speak. Their association is not sentimental, but practical, and is based on the fact that it is safer to hunt woodchucks in pairs than alone. These two dogs start out together in the morning, without a word, and come back together in the evening, when they part without saying good night, whether they have had any luck or not. Avoidance of farewells, which are always stuffy and some-times painful, is another thing in which it seems to me dogs have better sense than people.

22

Well, one day, the daughter, a dog about ten months old, seemed, by some prank of nature which again I am unable clearly to understand, for a moment or two to recognize her mother after all those months of oblivion. The two had just started out after a fat woodchuck who lived in the orchard. Something felt wrong with the daughter's ear—a long, floppy ear. "Mother," she said, "I wish you'd look at my ear."

Instantly the other dog bristled and growled. "I'm not your mother," she said. "I'm a woodchuck-hunter."

The daughter grinned. "Well," she said, just to show that there were no hard feelings, "that's not my ear, it's a shortstop's glove."

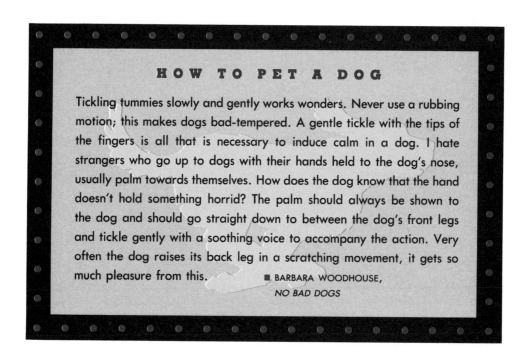

H O W   T O   P E T   A   D O G

Tickling tummies slowly and gently works wonders. Never use a rubbing motion; this makes dogs bad-tempered. A gentle tickle with the tips of the fingers is all that is necessary to induce calm in a dog. I hate strangers who go up to dogs with their hands held to the dog's nose, usually palm towards themselves. How does the dog know that the hand doesn't hold something horrid? The palm should always be shown to the dog and should go straight down to between the dog's front legs and tickle gently with a soothing voice to accompany the action. Very often the dog raises its back leg in a scratching movement, it gets so much pleasure from this. ■ BARBARA WOODHOUSE, *NO BAD DOGS*

To be sure, the dog is loyal. But why, on that account, should we take him as an example? He is loyal to men, not to other dogs.   KARL KRAUS

BODY AND SOUL

Once a dog has attached itself to a human, almost nothing can break the bond, as the following legends and anecdotes attest:

■

On a grave behind an iron fence in the town of Beddgelert in North Wales there stands a marker that recounts the legend of one Llewelyn, a thirteenth-century prince whose hound, Gelert, disappeared mysteriously one day as his master rode out to the hunt. When the prince returned, his infant son was nowhere to be found, the child's crib was overturned and bloody, and Gelert had blood dripping from his fangs. Convinced that the dog had devoured the baby, Prince Llewelyn drew his sword and plunged it into the dog. Gelert's dying cry awoke the sleeping child, who was concealed under the bedclothes. Hidden under the bed was the body of an enormous wolf . . . with its throat torn out.

■

Greyfriars Bobby was a Skye terrier who worked for a Scottish shepherd named Old Jock. In 1858, the day after Jock was buried in the churchyard at Greyfriars Abbey in Edinburgh, Bobby was found sleeping on his master's grave and was evicted from the graveyard. But Bobby returned day after day, in good weather and bad, to keep his vigil by the grave. The little dog eventually became a tourist attraction, with visitors from all over the world coming to see him and a local innkeeper feeding him every day. When Bobby died in 1872, church officials allowed him to be buried next to Jock, and a statue of Bobby—actually a drinking fountain for dogs—is an Edinburgh landmark to this day.

■

Scannon was a black Newfoundland who accompanied Meriwether Lewis on his exploration of the Louisiana Territory with William Clark. A skillful hunter and a fierce protector, Scannon saved three men when he deflected a charging buffalo. When Scannon was kidnapped by Indians, Lewis dispatched a search party with orders to kill the abductors, but the Indians abandoned the dog and fled when they saw their armed pursuers, and Scannon was reunited with his grateful master.

■

Marie Antoinette's spaniel, Thisbe, was so distraught when her mistress was executed that she jumped into the Seine and drowned.

■

Hachi, an Akita owned by a professor at Tokyo University, accompanied his master to the train station every morning and was there to greet him every evening upon his return. One day in 1925, Hachi waited as usual, but the professor had died while in town. Hachi nonetheless returned to the station the next day, and the next, and every day until his own death ten years later.

■

T.H. White, the author of *The Once and Future King*, was given an Irish setter bitch named Brownie in 1933, but it wasn't until four years later, while nursing her through a bout of distemper, that he realized he loved her. When Brownie died in 1944, White wrote in his journal: "She was a sprite who danced before me through twelve perfect years of love. . . . It means that I died last night. All that was me is dead." And he wrote to a friend that she was "more perfect than anything else in all my life . . . she was wife, mother, mistress and child . . . she was all I had."

He is our intimate and impassioned slave, whom nothing discourages, whom nothing repels, whose ardent trust and love nothing can impair. . . . His every instinct appears to think only of us; to serve us better; to adapt himself to our different needs. . . . He is the only living being that has found and recognizes an indubitable, tangible, and definite god. He knows to whom above him to give himself. He has not to seek for a superior and infinite power. . . . He has loyally, religiously, irrevocably recognized man's superiority and has surrendered himself to him, body and soul. . . .

■ MAURICE MAETERLINCK,
"OUR FRIEND, THE DOG"

Of all the animals, surely the dog is the only one that really shares our life, helps in our work, and has a place in our recreation. It is the only one that becomes so fond of us that sometimes it cannot go on living after its master dies.　　■ FERNAND MERCY

27

The man had saved his life, which was something; but, further, he was the ideal master. Other men saw to the welfare of their dogs from a sense of duty and business expediency; he saw to the welfare of his as if they were his own children, because he could not help it. And he saw further. He never forgot a kindly greeting or a cheering word, and to sit down for a long talk with them ("gas" he called it) was as much his delight as theirs. He had a way of taking Buck's head roughly between his hands and resting his own head upon Buck's, of shaking him back and forth, the while calling him ill names that to Buck were love names. Buck knew no greater joy than that rough embrace and the sound of murmured oaths, and at each jerk back and forth it seemed that his heart would be shaken out of his body, so great was his ecstasy. And when, released, he sprang to his feet, his mouth laughing, his eyes

With an unquestioning certainty, an unconstraint and a sim-
plicity that surprised us a little, deeming us better and more
powerful than all that exists, he betrays, for our benefit, the
whole of the animal kingdom to which he belongs and, without
scruple, denies his race, his kin, his mother and his young.

MAURICE MAETERLINCK,
"OUR FRIEND, THE DOG"

Los Angeles Times Photo by Brian Gadbery

eloquent, his throat vibrant with unuttered sound, and in that fashion remained without movement, John Thornton would reverently exclaim, "God! you can all but speak!"

■ JACK LONDON,
THE CALL OF THE WILD

Our dogs will love and admire the meanest of us, and feed our colossal vanity with their uncritical homage.

■ AGNES REPPLIER,
"THE IDOLATROUS DOG"

The fidelity of a dog is a precious gift demanding no less binding moral responsibilities than the friendship of a human being. The bond with a true dog is as lasting as the ties of this earth can ever be.

■ KONRAD LORENZ,
MAN MEETS DOG

I could never take dogs for granted. Why were they so devoted to the human race? Why should they delight in our company and welcome us home in transports of joy? Why should their greatest pleasure lie in being with us in our homes and wherever we were? They were just animals, after all, and it seemed to me that their main preoccupation ought to be in seeking food and protection; instead they dispensed a flow of affection and loyalty which appeared to be limitless.

■ JAMES HERRIOT,
JAMES HERRIOT'S DOG STORIES

You ask of my companions. Hills, sir, and the sundown, and a dog as large as myself that my father bought me. They are better than human beings, because they know but do not tell.

■ EMILY DICKINSON

We have not to gain his confidence or his friendship: he is born our friend; while his eyes are still closed, already he believes in us: even before his birth, he has given himself to man. But the word "friend" does not exactly depict his affectionate worship. He loves us and reveres us as though we had drawn him out of nothing.

■ MAURICE MAETERLINCK,
"OUR FRIEND, THE DOG"

Dogs understand your moods and your thoughts, and if you are thinking unpleasant things about your dog, he will pick it up and be downhearted.

■ BARBARA WOODHOUSE,
NO BAD DOGS

Sparky, a very cute, playful Cock-a-poo, is a member of a family whose dear son, Dimitri, lost his life in a car accident. Sparky actually "belonged" to the boy's younger brother, Damien, but Dimitri became especially attached to the dog and vice versa. Every day brought the two together in play. Dimitri was popular in school and active in sports. On the day following his tragic accident, many friends and teammates gathered at his home. Together with the family and their parish priest, they formed a circle, joined hands, and recited the Lord's Prayer. At that moment, Sparky came to the center of the healing circle, put back his head, and moaned in a totally uncharacteristic way. The sound he emitted had never been heard before, a very clear sound of grief— and comfort—to all present.

■ JULIE ADAMS CHURCH,
JOY IN A WOOLY COAT

My family's St. Bernard, Amy, weighed about a hundred and thirty pounds and hopped like a rabbit. The slobbering giant's only stroke of luck in her short life was to be purchased by sappy pet slaves and not by ruthless, Darwinian dog purists. For Amy had enough genetic dis-

Sensitive dogs are particularly gentle with the children of a
beloved master. It is as though they understand how much they
mean to him. Any fear that the dog may harm the children is
absurd.   KONRAD LORENZ,
                      MAN MEETS DOG

orders to be Euthanasia Poster Dog, and our family's finances took a beating each time a new one showed up. As a child, I was awed by Amy's many exotic ailments. The x-rays diagnosing Amy's hip dysplasia (source of the bunny hop) were sent to the University of Pennsylvania vet school for analysis. No one else in our family ever consulted specialists. A few years later, she required expensive plastic surgery to fix inverted eyelids. But the worst of her genetic problems, and the one that made her my family's most beloved pet ever, was her inbred stupidity. Somehow she managed to get hit by a car on a country road that saw maybe three vehicles every hour. After paying the vet bill to fix a complicated fracture, my parents happily took her home and then went about devising a system to walk Amy outside, which required all four family members to first hoist her up with a canvas log-carrier and then coordinate leading her while swinging her cast along. I'm sure that if a motorized wheelchair had been available for canines back then, my parents would have rented one.

Amy died a genetically appropriate death, at the age of six, by succumbing to a stomach ailment common in large breeds. One day after she ate her dinner, her stomach flipped over, causing gangrene to set in. My father rushed her to the vet on a plywood stretcher, but it was too late. The night of that silly dog's death was the only time I ever saw my father cry. ■ C.E. CRIMMINS

Immediately after Mary Queen of Scots was beheaded, a strange and pathetic memorial to that devotion which she had always aroused in those who knew her intimately, was discovered: Her little lap dog, a Skye terrier, who had managed to accompany her under her long skirts, had now crept out from beneath her petticoats and in its distress, had stationed itself between the severed head and the shoulders of the body. Nor could it be coaxed away, but steadfastly and uncomprehendingly

clung to the solitary thing that it could find which still reminded it of its dead mistress. ■ ANTONIA FRASER,
MARY QUEEN OF SCOTS

Scott always talked to [his dog] Camp as if he understood what was said—and the animal certainly did understand not a little of it; it seemed as if he perfectly comprehended that his master considered him as a sensible and steady friend.
■ J.G. LOCKHART,
LIFE OF SIR WALTER SCOTT

Gentlemen of the jury, the best friend a man has in the world may turn against him and become his worst enemy. His son or daughter that he has reared with loving care may prove ungrateful. Those who are nearest and dearest to us, those whom we trust with our happiness and our good name, may become traitors to their faith. The money that a man has, he may lose. It flies away from him, perhaps when he needs it the most. A man's reputation may be sacrificed in a moment of ill-considered action. The people who are prone to fall on their knees to do us honor when success is with us may be the first to throw the stone of malice when failure settles its cloud upon our heads. The one absolutely unselfish friend that a man can have in this selfish world, the one that never deserts him and the one that never proves ungrateful or treacherous is his dog.

   Gentlemen of the jury . . . when riches take wings and reputation falls to pieces, he is as constant in his love as the sun in its journey through the heavens. If fortune drives the master forth an outcast in the world, friendless and homeless, the faithful dog asks no higher privilege than that of accompanying him to guard against danger, to fight against his enemies, and when the last scene of all comes, and death takes the master in its embrace and his body is laid away in the cold ground, no

33

matter if all other friends pursue their way, there by his graveside will the noble dog be found, his head between his paws, his eyes sad but open in alert watchfulness, faithful and true even to death.

■ GEORGE GRAHAM VEST,
CHARLES BURDEN,
RESPONDENT V. LEONIDAS HORNSBY,
APPELLANT (1870), A SUIT FOR DAM-
AGES BY THE OWNER OF A DOG SHOT
FOR TRESPASSING

Watch came round and placed himself square before his master and deposited the lost spectacles before his feet. He had found them in the turnip-field over a mile from home, and though but a dog, he remembered that he had seen them on people's noses and in their hands, and knew that they must therefore be valuable—not to himself, but to that larger and more important kind of dog that goes about on its hind legs.

■ W.H. HUDSON,
A SHEPHERD'S LIFE

The owner of a Doberman pinscher fell 250 feet down a steep canyon wall in a futile attempt to reach his pet, and rescue crews were unable to reach the animal, who was killed in a 325-foot fall. The man and his dog had been hiking in a remote area of Los Angeles County. "He was like my brother," said the man. "I can't just leave him there. . . . I owe it to him to bury him. I feel like I let him down. He felt safe with me and I was leading him. Leading him to his death."

■ *THE LOS ANGELES TIMES*

Brothers and sisters, I bid you beware
Of giving your heart to a dog to tear.

■ RUDYARD KIPLING,
THE POWER OF THE DOG

Dogs are seldom jealous of small children. The mind of a dog looks upon small children as it would look upon its own whelps. That is why even fierce dogs are seldom known to hurt children.

BARBARA WOODHOUSE,
NO BAD DOGS

GAGA

According to a recent survey, ninety-one percent of dog owners speak baby talk to their dogs and buy them holiday gifts. Many of them carry photos of their dogs, talk to them on the phone, and send them postcards.

■

An Illinois government official whose dog died as the result of eating a tampon appointed a special prosecutor to investigate the incident. The veterinarian who treated the animal had his license suspended for forty-five days.

■

A man in Massachusetts painted black spots on his white car to match his six-year-old Dalmation.

■

The Duchess of York is reported to have "knighted" her dog, Rutherford, with a dinner knife.

■

A nondenominational clergyman in Denver, Colorado, claims to have married a couple who used a dog as a ring bearer.

MONDO
CANINE

And there's a wide variety of products and services available to dotty dog owners:

- all kinds of gustatory delights, including "gourmet" biscuits and "Thirsty Pup" bottled water for dogs;
- hand-painted, custom-tailored canine apparel;
- doggie portraits starting at $300, your dog's image on note paper;
- The Pet Limo in Beverly Hills, for those who want their dogs transported "safely, comfortably and courteously";
- portable ramps to help disabled dogs climb to a favorite resting spot;
- a pet psychic in Los Angeles who specializes in dogs;
- a dog psychiatrist in Massachusetts who makes house calls;
- cosmetic surgery to remove patches of unsightly hair;
- a Florida company that will freeze-dry Fido for posterity.

The rich and famous seem especially inclined to such extreme attachment and indulgence:

- Henry III of France carried his small dog around with him everywhere in a basket hung around his neck.
- Sir Walter Scott's Maida, a greyhound-mastiff mix, sat at the dinner table and posed for portraits with his master.
- Josephine insisted on allowing her small dog to sleep in the imperial bed over Napoleon's strenuous—and futile—objections.
- Elizabeth Barrett Browning's red cocker spaniel, Flush, was the subject of two of her poems and a biography by Virginia Woolf. He was kidnapped several times, but she always got him back—after paying ransom.
- Giuseppe Verdi's Maltese spaniel, Lulu, accompanied the composer everywhere concealed under his coat and served as a sounding board for his new compositions. After Lulu died, Verdi complained that he

MONDO
CANINE

could no longer write opera without his little "colleague." He had her buried just outside his bedroom window.

■ T.H. White made many sacrifices for his Irish setter, Brownie. He couldn't go to libraries because she was barred from them, which was his only real regret, since he hardly missed going to the cinema, the theater, or other public places. He said that she "disapproved" of his absence for more than a few minutes. White's poem, "Off to the Wars," is addressed to Brownie:

> Brownie, my Brownie, now that I am going—
> This may be no good poem, but it will be truth—
> You have been to me mother and daughter,
> Decency, kindness, love, beauty and youth.
> Forget me then. Oh, forget me utterly.
> Forget quick and be happy and live long.
> If you remember for a minute, I shall die in badness,
> Or live in ashes and beastly, remorseful, wrong.
> Live you, tail flirting, eyes pleading,
> In pleasure, in brownness, in trust of my race.
> Only thus shall I live or die, my darling,
> Not in disgrace.

■ The novelist Ellen Glasgow was gaga over her two dogs, Billy and Jeremy, whom she often addressed as "Mr. Billy Bennett" and "Mr. Jeremy Glasgow." She sent them postcards when she was away from home and had collars and clothing custom made for them in London.

■ Winston Churchill wrote these lines when his daughter Mary's pug was ill:

> Oh, what is the matter with poor Puggy-wug?
> Pet him and kiss him and give him a hug.

Run and fetch him a suitable drug,
Wrap him up tenderly all in a rug,
That is the way to cure Puggy-wug.

- At Chequers one evening, while the film *Oliver Twist* was being shown, Churchill's poodle, Rufus, was seated on his master's lap as usual. Just as Bill Sikes is about to drown his dog in the film, Churchill covered Rufus's eyes and said, "Don't look now, dear. I'll tell you about it afterwards."
- U.S. Senator Robert Byrd read a two-page greeting to his Maltese terriers, Billy and Bonnie, into the *Congressional Record*—at a cost to the taxpayers of $1,000.

American oil heiress Eleanor Ritchey died in 1968, leaving $5 million to the 150 stray dogs she kept on her ranch in Fort Lauderdale, Florida. The will was contested, but the dogs won; they remained on the ranch under the care of Ritchey's former chauffeur, who had driven her around in a Cadillac picking up the dogs. Musketeer, the last of the pack, died in 1984; the estate passed to the Auburn University Research Foundation. . . . The wealthiest dog on record is Toby, a standard Poodle who was left over $30 million by his owner, Miss Ella Wendel. During Wendel's lifetime, Toby slept on silk sheets in his own bedroom and was served breakfast in bed by a butler. After her death, despite his fortune, Toby was forced to sleep in a wooden box in the kitchen and eat his meals on the floor. Sadly, he was put to sleep by the bickering executors of the will.   ■ WAYNE KIRN,
1990 365 DOGS CALENDAR

Estimated number of American dogs that have been named as beneficiaries in wills: 1,000,000.

■ *HARPER'S INDEX*

MONDO
CANINE

Richard Hartog/The Outlook

[Joe Wright, J.R.R. Tolkien's professor of Comparative Philology at Oxford] married a former pupil. Two children were born to them, but both died in infancy. Nevertheless the Wrights carried on a stoic and lively existence in a huge house built to Joe's design in the Banbury Road. In 1912 Ronald Tolkien came to Wright as a pupil, and ever afterwards remembered "the vastness of Joe Wright's dining-room table, when I sat alone at one end learning the elements of Greek philology from glinting glasses in the further gloom." Nor was he ever likely to forget the huge Yorkshire teas given by the Wrights on Sunday afternoons, when Joe would cut gargantuan slices from a heavyweight plum cake, and Jack the Aberdeen terrier would perform his party trick of licking his lips noisily when his master pronounced the Gothic word for fig tree, *smakka-bagms*. ■ HUMPHREY CARPENTER,
TOLKIEN: A BIOGRAPHY

42

D O G   N A M E S

Canine cognomens should be designed to impinge on the ears of dogs
and not to amuse neighbors, tradespeople, and casual visitors.

> ■ JAMES THURBER,
> *"HOW TO NAME A DOG"*

Half the handsome spaniels in England are called Dash, just as half the
tall footmen are called Thomas.

> ■ M.R. MITFORD,
> *OUR VILLAGE*

The five most popular dog names in America:
Duke
Brandy
Max
Sam
Shadow   ■ PURINA DOG CHOW SURVEY

We called him Old Yeller. The name had a sort of double meaning.
One part meant that his short hair was a dingy yellow, a color that we
called "yeller" in those days. The other meant that when he opened his
head, the sound he let out came closer to being a yell than a bark.

> ■ FRED GIPSON,
> *OLD YELLER*

He was the biggest fool-pup I ever saw, chock full of life and spirits,
always going at racing speed, generally into mischief, breaking his
heart if his master did not notice him, chewing up clothing, digging up
garden stuff, going direct from a wallow in the pigsty to frolic in the

baby's cradle, getting kicked in the ribs by horses and tossed by cows, but still the same hilarious, rollicking, good-natured, energetic fool-pup, and given by common consent the fit name of Silly Billy.

■ ERNEST THOMPSON SETON,
"THE MAKING OF SILLY BILLY"

We had called the dog Stranger out of the faint hope that he was just passing through. As it turned out, the name was most inappropriate since he stayed on for nearly a score of years, all the while biting the hands that fed him and making snide remarks about my grandmother's cooking. Eventually the name was abbreviated to "Strange," which was shorter and much more descriptive.

■ PATRICK F. McMANUS,
"A DOG FOR ALL SEASONS"

[Duke was] no beauty, but [he] certainly deserved the name better than those who had assumed it.

■ JEAN JACQUES ROUSSEAU,
CONFESSIONS

Dear Lytton Strachey, Some time in 1913, at this address, my wife and I acquired a young fox-terrier. We debated as to what to call him, and, as Henry James had just been having his seventieth birthday, and as his books had given me more pleasure than those of any other living man, I, rather priggishly perhaps, insisted that the dog should be known as James. But this was a name which Italian peasants, who are the only neighbours we have, of course would not be able to pronounce at all. So we were phonetic and called the name of the dog *Yah-mes*. And this did very well. By this name he was known far and wide—but not for long; for alas, he died of distemper.

■ MAX BEERBOHM,
LETTERS OF MAX BEERBOHM 1892–1956

MONDO
CANINE

I know a hunter who changed his dog's name. His first mistake was to let his young daughter name the pup. She named the setter Lovely Lady, and she was. The hunter trained the pup. On the first trip with his hunting cronies, the pup decided to investigate the world. Angered by her misbehavior, the hunter took off, hell-bent-for-election, crashing through the woods, calling the dog at the top of his voice—LOVELY LADY—LOVELY LADY. . . .

■ RICHARD A. WOLTERS,
GUN DOG

When I sit reading in a corner of the garden wall, or on the lawn with my back to a favorite tree, I enjoy interrupting my intellectual preoccupations to talk and play with Bashan. And what do I say to him? Mostly his own name, the two syllables which are of the utmost personal interest because they refer to himself and have an electric effect upon his whole being. I rouse and stimulate his sense of his own ego by impressing upon him—varying my tone and emphasis—that he *is* Bashan and that Bashan is his name. By continuing this for a while I can actually produce in him a state of ecstasy, a sort of intoxication with his own identity, so that he begins to whirl round on himself and send up loud exultant barks to heaven out of the weight of dignity that lies on his chest.

■ THOMAS MANN,
"BASHAN"

45

D O G   D A Y S

K O N R A D   L O R E N Z

The brilliant smell of water,
The brave smell of a stone
■ G. K. CHESTERTON:
"QUOODLE'S SONG"

I do not know how the dog days got their name.

I believe from Sirius the dog star, but the etymological origin of the North German synonym, the *Saueregurkenzeit* (sour cucumber time), seems much more appropriate. But for me personally, the dog days could not be better named, because I make a habit of spending them in the exclusive company of my dog. When I am fed to the teeth with brain work, when clever talk and politeness nearly drive me distracted, when the very sight of a typewriter fills me with revulsion, all of which sentiments generally overtake me at the end of a normal summer term, then I decide to "go to the dogs." I retire from human society and seek that of animals—and for this reason: I know almost no human being who is lazy enough to keep me company in such a mood, for I possess the priceless gift of being able, when in a state of great contentment, to shut off my higher thinking powers completely, and this is the essential condition for perfect peace of mind. When, on a hot summer day, I swim across the Danube and lie in a dreamy backwater of the great river, like a crocodile in the mud, among scenery that shows not the slightest sign of the existence of human civilization, then

I sometimes achieve that miraculous state which is the highest goal of oriental sages. Without going to sleep, my higher centers dissolve into a strange at-oneness with surrounding nature; my thoughts stand still, time ceases to mean anything and, when the sun begins to sink and the cool of the evening warns me that I have still another three and a half miles to swim home, I do not know whether seconds or years have passed since I crawled out on to the muddy bank.

This animal nirvana is an unequaled panacea for mental strain, true balm for the mind of hurried, worried modern Man, which has been rubbed sore in so many places. I do not always succeed in achieving this healing return to the thoughtless happiness of prehuman paradise but I am most likely to do so in the company of an animal which is still a rightful participant of it. Thus there are very definite and deep-rooted reasons why I need a dog which accompanies me faithfully but which has retained a wild exterior and thus does not spoil the landscape by its civilized appearance.

Yesterday morning at dawn—it was already so hot that work, mental work, seemed hopeless, a heaven-sent Danube day!—I left my room, armed with fishing net and glass jar in order to catch and carry the live food I always bring home for my fishes from every Danube excursion. As always, this is an unmistakable sign for Susi that a dog day, a happy dog day is pending. She is quite convinced that I undertake these expeditions for her exclusive benefit and perhaps she is not altogether wrong. She knows I not only allow her to go with me but that I set the greatest store by her company. Nevertheless, to be quite sure of not being left behind, she presses close to my legs all the way to the yard gate. Then, with proudly raised bushy tail, she trots down the village street before me, her dancing, elastic gait showing all the village dogs that she is afraid of none of them, even when Wolf II is not with her. With the horribly ugly mongrel belonging to the village grocer—I hope he will never read this book—she usually has a short flirtation. To the deep disgust of Wolf II, she loves this checkered creature more than any other dog, but today she has no time for him, and when he attempts to play with her she wrinkles her nose and bares her gleaming teeth at him before trotting on to growl, according to her custom, at her various enemies behind their different garden fences.

The village street is still in the shade and its hard ground is cold beneath my bare feet, but beyond the railway bridge, the deep dust of the path to the river presses itself, caressingly warm, between my toes, and above the footprints of the dog trotting in front of me it rises in little clouds in the still air. Crickets and cicada chirp merrily and, on the nearby riverbank, a golden oriole and a black-cap are singing. Thank goodness that they are still singing—that summer is still young enough. Our way leads over a freshly mown meadow and Susi leaves the path, for this is a special "mousing" meadow. Her trot becomes a curious, stiff-legged slink, she carries her head very high, her whole expression betraying her excitement, and her tail sinks low, stretched out behind, close above the ground. Altogether she resembles a rather too fat blue Arctic fox. Suddenly, as though released by a spring, she shoots in a semicircle about a yard high and two yards forward. Landing on her forepaws close together and stiffly outstretched, she bites several times quick as lightning, into the short grass. With loud snorts she bores her pointed nose into the ground, then, raising her head, she looks questioningly in my direction, her tail wagging all the time: the mouse has gone. She certainly feels ashamed when her tremendous mouse jump misses its mark, and she is equally proud if she catches her prey. Now she slinks farther on and four further leaps fall short of their goal—voles are amazingly quick and agile. But now the little chow bitch flies through the air like a rubber ball, and as her paws touch the ground, there follows a high-pitched, painfully sharp squeak. She bites again, then, with a hurried shaking movement, drops what she was biting, and a small gray body flies in a semicircle through the air with Susi, in a larger semicircle, after it. Snapping several times with retracted lips, she seizes, with her incisors only, something squeaking and struggling in the grass. Then she turns to me and shows me the big, fat, distorted fieldmouse that she is holding in her jaws. I praise her roundly and declare that she is a most terrifying, awe-inspiring animal for whom one must have the greatest respect. I am sorry for the vole, but I did not know it personally, and Susi is my bosom friend whose triumphs I feel bound to share. Nevertheless, my conscience is easier when she eats it, thereby vindicating herself by the only action that can ever justify killing. First she gingerly chews it with her incisors only to a formless but still intact mass,

48

MONDO
CANINE

then she takes it far back into her mouth and begins to gobble it up and swallow it. And now for the time being she has had enough of mousing and suggests to me that we should proceed.

Our path leads to the river, where I undress and hide my clothes and fishing tackle. From here the track goes upstream, following the old towpath where in former times horses used to pull the ships up the river. But now the path is overgrown, till only a narrow strip remains which leads through a thick forest of goldenrod, mixed unpleasantly with solitary nettles and blackberry bushes, so that one needs both arms to keep the stinging, pricking vegetation from one's body. The damp heat in this plant wilderness is truly unbearable and Susi walks panting at my heels, quite indifferent to any hunting prospects that the undergrowth may hold. I can understand her apathy because I am dripping with sweat, and I pity her in her thick fur coat. At last we reach the place where I wish to cross the river. At the present low level of the river a wide shingle bank stretches far out into the current and, as I pick my way somewhat painfully over the stones, Susi runs ahead joyfully and plunges breast high into the water, where she lies down until only her head remains visible, a queer little angular outline against the vast expanse of the river.

As I wade out into the current, the dog presses close behind me and whines softly. She has never yet crossed the Danube, and its width fills her with misgiving. I speak reassuringly to her and wade in farther, but she is obliged to start swimming when the water reaches barely to my knees and she is carried rapidly downstream. In order to keep up with her, I begin to swim too, although it is far too shallow for me, but the fact that I am now traveling as swiftly as she is reassures her and she swims steadily by my side. A dog that will swim alongside its master shows particular intelligence: many dogs can never realize the fact that in the water a man is not upright as it is used to seeing him, with the unpleasant result that in an attempt to keep close behind the head on the surface of the water, it scratches its master's back horribly with wildly paddling paws.

But Susi has immediately grasped the fact that a man swims horizontally and she carefully avoids coming too near to me from behind. She is nervous in the broad sweeping river and keeps as close beside me as possible. Now her anxiety reaches such a pitch that she rears up out of the water and looks back at the bank we have left behind us. I am afraid that she may turn back altogether, but she settles down again, swimming quietly at my side. Soon another difficulty arises: in her excitement and in the effort to cross the great wide current as quickly as possible, she strikes out at a speed which I cannot indefinitely maintain. Panting, I strain to keep up with her, but she outstrips me again and again, only to turn round and swim back to me every time she finds herself a few yards ahead. There is always the danger that, on sighting our home shore, she will leave me and return to it, since for an animal in a state of apprehension the direction of home exerts a much stronger pull than any other. In any case, dogs find it hard to alter course while swimming, so I am relieved when I have persuaded her to turn again in the right direction and, swimming with all my might to keep close behind her, to send her on again each time she tries to come back. The fact that she understands my encouragement and is influenced by it is fresh proof to me that her intelligence is well above the average.

We land on a sandbank that is steeper than the one we have just left. Susi is some yards in front of me, and as she climbs out of the water and makes her first few steps on dry land I see that she sways noticeably to and fro. This slight disturbance of balance, which passes in a few seconds and which I myself often experience after a longer swim, is known to many swimmers, who have confirmed my observation. But I can find no satisfactory physiological explanation for it. Although I have repeatedly noticed it in dogs, I have never seen it in such a marked degree as Susi showed on this occasion. The condition has nothing to do with exhaustion, which fact Susi at once makes clear to me by expressing in no uncertain measure her joy at having conquered the stream. She bursts forth in an ecstasy of joy, races in small circles round my legs and finally fetches a stick for me to throw for her, a game into which I willingly enter. When she grows tired of it, she rushes off at top speed after a wagtail which is sitting on the shore some fifty yards away; not that she naïvely expects to catch the bird, for she knows quite well that wagtails like to fly along the riverbank and that when they have gained a few dozen yards they sit down again, thus making excellent pacemakers for a short hunt.

I am glad that my little friend is in such a happy mood, for it means much to me that she should often come on these swimming expeditions across the Danube. For this reason, I wish to reward her amply for her first crossing of the river, and there is no better way of doing this than by taking her for a long walk through the delightful virgin wilderness flanking the shores of the river. One can learn a lot when wandering through this wilderness with an animal friend, particularly if one lets oneself be guided by its tastes and interests.

First we walk upstream along the river's edge, then we follow the course of a little backwater which, at its lower end, is clear and deep; farther on, it breaks up into a chain of little pools, which become shallower and shallower as we proceed. A strangely tropical effect is produced by these backwaters. The banks descend in wild luxuriance, steeply, almost vertically, to the water, and are begirt by a regular botanical garden of high willows, poplars and oaks, between which hang dense strands of lush wood vine, like lianas; kingfishers, and golden orioles, also typical denizens of this land-scape, both belong to groups of birds, the majority of whose members are tropical dwellers. In the water grows thick swamp vegetation. Tropical too is the damp heat which hangs over this wonderful jungle landscape, which can only be borne with comfort and dignity by a naked man who spends more time in the water than out of it; and finally, let us not deny that malaria mosquitoes and numerous gadflies play their part in enhancing the tropical impression.

51

In the broad band of mud that frames the backwater, the tracks of many riverside dwellers can be seen, as though cast in plaster, and their visiting cards are printed in the hard-baked clay until the next rainfall or high water. Who has contended that there are no more stags in the Danube swamps? Judging by the hoofprints, there must still be many large ones, although they are scarcely ever heard at rutting time, so furtive have they become since the perils of the last war, whose final, terrible phases took place in these very woods. Foxes and deer, muskrats and smaller rodents, countless common sandpipers, wood sandpipers and little ringed plovers have deco-rated the mud with the interwoven chains of their footsteps. And if these tracks are full of interest for my eyes, how much more so must they be for the nose of my little chow bitch! She revels in scent orgies of which we poor noseless ones can have no conception, for "Goodness only knows the noselessness of Man." The tracks of stags and large deer do not interest her, for, thank heaven, Susi is no big game hunter, being far too obsessed with her passion for mousing.

But the scent of a muskrat is a different thing; slinking tremulously, her nose close to the ground and her tail stretched obliquely upward and backward, she follows these rodents to the very entrance of their burrows, which, owing to the present low water, are above instead of below the water line. She applies her nose to the holes, greedily inhaling the delicious smell of game, and she even begins the hopeless task of digging up the burrow, which pleasure I do not deny her. I lie flat on my stomach, in the hand-deep, lukewarm water, letting the sun burn down on my back, and I am in no hurry to move on. At last Susi turns toward me a face plastered with earth; wagging her tail, she walks panting toward me and with a deep sigh lies down beside me in the water. So we remain for nearly an hour, at the end of which time she gets up and begs me to go on. We pursue the ever drier course of the backwater upstream, and now, as we turn a bend and find another pool, quite unconscious of our presence— for the wind is against us—is a huge muskrat: the apotheosis of all Susi's dreams, a gigantic, a godlike rat, a rat of unprecedented dimensions. The dog freezes to a statue and I do likewise. Then, slowly as a chameleon, step by step, she begins to stalk the wonder beast. She gets amazingly far, covering almost half the distance which separates us from the rat; and it is tremendously thrilling, for there is always the chance that, in its first bewilderment, it may jump into the pool, which has shrunk away into its stony bed and has no outlet. The creature's burrow must be at least some yards away from the spot, on the level of the normal water line. But I have underestimated the intelligence of the rat. All of a sudden he sees the dog and streaks like lightning across the mud in the direction of the bank, Susi after him like a shot from a gun. She is clever enough not to pursue him in a straight line but to try to cut him off at a tangent, on his way to cover. Simultaneously she lets out a passionate cry such as I have rarely heard from a dog. Perhaps if she had not given tongue and had instead applied her whole energy to the chase, she might have got him, for she is but half a yard behind as he disappears into safety.

Expecting Susi to dig for ages at the mouth of the earth, I lie down in the mud of the pool, but she only sniffs longingly at the entrance, then turns away disappointedly and rejoins me in the water. We both feel that the day has reached its climax: golden orioles sing, frogs croak, and great dragonflies, with a dry whirr of their glossy wings, chase the gadflies which are tormenting us. Good luck to their hunting! So we lie nearly all afternoon and I succeed in being more animal than any animal or at any rate much lazier than my dog, in fact as lazy as any crocodile. This bores Susi and, having nothing better to do, she begins to chase the frogs which, made bold by our long inertia, have resumed their activities. She stalks the nearest one, trying out her mouse-jump technique in the attempt to kill this new prey. But her paws land with a splash in the water and the frog dives away unhurt. Shaking the water from her eyes, she looks around to see where the frog has got to. She sees it, or thinks she does, in the middle of the pool where the rounded shoots of a water mint appear, to the imperfect eyesight of a dog, not unlike the head of a squatting frog. Susi eyes the object, holding her head first on the left side then on the right, then slowly, very slowly, she wades into the water, swims up to the plant and bites at it. Looking round with a long-suffering air to see if I am laughing at her absurd mistake, she turns about and finally swims back to the bank and lies down beside me. I ask, "Shall we go home?" and Susi springs up, answering "Yes" with all her available means of expression. We push our way through the jungle, straight ahead to the river. We are a long way upstream from Altenberg, but the current carries us at the rate of nearly twelve miles an hour. Susi shows no more fear of the great expanse of water, and she swims quietly beside me, letting the stream carry her along. We land close by my clothes and fishing tackle and hastily I catch a delicious supper for the fish in my aquaria. Then in the dusk, satisfied and happy, we return home the same way as we came. In the mousing meadow, Susi has better luck, for she catches no less than three fat voles in succession—a compensation for her failure with the muskrat and the frog.

Today I must go to Vienna, although the heat forecasts another "dog day." I must take this chapter to the publisher. No, Susi, you cannot come with me, you can see I've got long trousers on. But tomorrow, tomorrow, Susi, we'll swim the Danube again and, if we try very hard, perhaps we'll even catch that muskrat.

SOME BREEDS

ABERDEEN TERRIER

Aberdeen terriers are intelligent and (if you don't mind those beetling eyebrows) handsome, but so austere and full of the Calvinistic spirit that it is impossible for an ordinary erring human being not to feel ill at ease in their presence.   P.G. WODEHOUSE

AIREDALE TERRIER

Right-thinking people know in their hearts that terriers are a superior dog, a breed apart, and the Airedale is the king of terriers: foe of rats, loyal but not slavish, independent but not haughty, involved without being overeager, strong but never bullying. They meet the world head-on with an unrivaled mixture of style, brains, and clownish wit, the very ingredients one looks for in a spouse.

■ CHIP BROWN

An Airedale can do anything any other dog can do and then whip the other dog if he has to.   ■ THEODORE ROOSEVELT

ALASKAN HUSKY

Their brain [is] like a piece of river rock.

■ JERRY RILEY IN
CLOSE FRIENDS
BY PETER JENKINS

MONDO
CANINE

AMERICAN PIT BULL TERRIER

Bull terriers are curious dogs, and one has to be a little kinky to like them. The majority of people, unfortunately, regard them as ruthless killers and a disgrace to the canine world.

■ JUNE KAY,
THE THIRTEENTH MOON

A disproportionately large number of pit bulls are able to climb trees.

■ RICHARD STRATTON

BASENJI

Dog trainers tested various breeds to see how they behaved under various circumstances. . . . In initiative requiring individual action—firecrackers set off near a litter of pups—the barkless African Basenji performed the best. Bit the fellow who lit the firecrackers.

■ L.M. BOYD

BASSET HOUND

The basset hound is a caricaturist's version of a beagle.

■ BERTON AVERRE

BLOODHOUND

I am the dog world's best detective.
My sleuthing nose is so effective
I sniff the guilty at a distance,
And then they lead a doomed existence.

■ EDWARD ANTHONY,
"THE BLOODHOUND"

He is a large, enormously evident creature, likely to make a housewife fear for her antiques and draperies, and he is not given to frolic and parlour games. He is used to the outdoors. If you want a dog to chase a stick or a ball, or jump through a hoop, don't look at him.

■ JAMES THURBER,
"LO, HEAR THE GENTLE BLOODHOUND!"

BORDER COLLIE

Border collies are very bright, quick and more than a little weird. They are not suitable for most city apartments. Their working instincts are strong and their self-esteem comes from working well. A bored, mis-handled Border collie can get into awful trouble.

■ DONALD McCAIG,
NOP'S TRIALS

BRITTANY SPANIEL

Brittanys were bred as poacher's dogs and lived almost literally in their master's hip pocket for generations. They were an extension of the old rogue's arm, trained to look innocent and unprepossessing, all the time plotting, thinking, scheming to make game.

■ JOEL M. VANCE

BULLDOG

The nose of the bulldog has been slanted backwards so that he can breathe without letting go.   ■ WINSTON CHURCHILL

DACHSHUND

Some day, if I ever get a chance, I shall write a book, or warning, on the character and temperament of the dachshund and why he can't be trained and shouldn't be. I would rather train a striped zebra to balance an Indian club than induce a dachshund to heed my slightest command.
■ E.B. WHITE

Dachshunds are ideal dogs for small children, as they are already stretched and pulled to such a length that the child cannot do much harm one way or the other. ■ ROBERT BENCHLEY

FOX TERRIER

Fox terriers are born with about four times as much original sin in them as other dogs. ■ JEROME K. JEROME

GREAT DANE

Things that upset a terrier may pass virtually unnoticed by a Great Dane. ■ SMILEY BLANTON

GREYHOUND

Greyhounds are pure carnivores. When they chase the hare at a race it's not for fun—they literally want to tear it to pieces.
■ PHIL REES

IRISH SETTER

He's been bred for his beauty, and as a result he's not worth the price of dog food to a hunter. His pointing instinct has been neglected and replaced by his fine red coat.

■ RICHARD A. WOLTERS,
HOME DOG

[The show-strain Irish and English Setters] have everything wrong that man can breed into a dog. In the field they are flat-footed, hip-crippled, stiff-backed, short-winded, overheated, ear-torn, eye-infected, and drooly-jowled. They are as hapless as the trout produced by fish hatcheries.

■ DATUS C. PROPER,
PHEASANTS OF THE MIND

They're so dumb they get lost on the end of their leash.

■ DR. MICHAEL FOX

58

LABRADOR RETRIEVER

All Labradors look rather friendly and pleased with themselves and with the world at large. Labradors acting as guides (for the blind) look not only pleased but confident, patient, and slightly self-important.

■ JO GRIMOND

Labradors [make] lousy watchdogs. They usually bark when there is a stranger about, but it is an expression of unmitigated joy at the chance to meet somebody new, not a warning.

■ NORMAN STRUNG

I got an early impression of retrievers when a friend would mark an orange with his fingernail and then throw it on top of a truck full of oranges. Then he'd call his Labrador, who would climb onto the truck, pick up the marked orange and bring it back. Good demostration, although I have since learned that the strong human scent makes this easy for a dog with a good nose.

■ CHARLEY WATERMAN,
GUN DOGS & BIRD GUNS

MALAMUTE

Malamutes, some of them, can sleep like nothing else that's animate. Convinced that there is nothing on earth that wants to hurt them, they can drop off in the middle of noise and crowds and sleep like cinder blocks.

■ DANIEL PINKWATER,
"ARNOLD COMES HOME"

MASTIFF

59

A mastiff dog
May love a puppy cur for no more reason
Than the twain have been tied up together.

■ ALFRED LORD TENNYSON,
"QUEEN MARY"

MONGREL

One is probably less likely to obtain in a mongrel a nervous, mentally deficient animal than in a dog with eight champions in its pedigree.

■ KONRAD LORENZ,
MAN MEETS DOG

Most cross-bred dogs have a thing called hybrid vigor which helps them fight disease.

■ JAMES HERRIOT,
"WES"

MONDO
CANINE

I like a bit of mongrel myself, whether it's a man or a dog; they're the best for everyday. ■ GEORGE BERNARD SHAW

NEWFOUNDLAND

Newfoundland dogs are good to save children from drowning, but you must have a pond of water handy and a child, or else there will be no profit in boarding a Newfoundland.
■ JOSH BILLINGS

PEKINGESE

Many people, I know, disparage Pekes, but take it from me, they are all right. If they have a fault, it is a tendency to think too much of themselves. ■ P.G. WODEHOUSE

A Pekingese is not a pet dog; he is an undersized lion.
■ A.A. MILNE

Pekes
Are biological freaks. ■ E.B. WHITE

If you have ever slept with a snoring Peke, a man sounds really good.
■ ROBIN HAMBRO

PHARAOH HOUND

The Pharaoh hound is the only breed of dog that blushes—or needs to: Pharaoh hounds have filthy minds.
■ HOWARD OGDEN,
PENSAMENTOES

MONDO CANINE

POODLE

I have never known, or even heard of, a bad poodle. Theirs is the most charming of species, including the human, and they happily lack Man's aggression, quick temper, and wild aim. They have courage, too, and they fight well and fairly when they have to fight. The poodle, moving into battle, lowers its head, attacks swiftly, and finishes the business without idle rhetoric or false innuendo.

■ JAMES THURBER,
"CHRISTABEL: PART ONE"

Poodles always listen attentively while being scolded, looking innocent, bewildered and misunderstood.

■ JAMES THURBER,
LANTERNS AND LANCES

I wonder if other dogs think poodles are members of a weird religious cult.
■ RITA RUDNER

PUG

The dog's tail and ears have been sent downstairs to be washed; from which circumstances we infer that the animal is no more. His forelegs have been delivered to the boots to be brushed, which strengthens the supposition.
■ CHARLES DICKENS,
SKETCHES BY BOZ

The pug is living proof that God has a sense of humor.
■ MARGO KAUFMAN

SEALYHAM TERRIER

A Sealyham's love of fun and his fidelity to his master can prove a real moral support to a melancholy type of person. Who can help laughing when such an amusing little creature, bursting with the joys of life, comes bouncing along with his far too short legs (walking teats, as a Sealyham-owning friend of mine calls them), cocks his head and, with an expression half knowing and half innocent, looks up at his master, inviting him to play?
■ KONRAD LORENZ,
MAN MEETS DOG

SCOTTISH TERRIER

They have all the compactness of a small dog and all the valor of a big one. And they are so exceedingly sturdy that it is proverbial that the only thing fatal to them is being run over by an automobile—in which case the car itself knows that it has been in a fight.
■ DOROTHY PARKER,
"TOWARD THE DOG DAYS"

A man once told me of two Scottish terriers, father and son, which entered a burrow through two separate openings. Underground in the darkness they encountered each other and each mistook the other for the quarry. They met in a terrible fight that ended in the death of both.
■ MAZO DE LA ROCHE,
PORTRAIT OF A DOG

SHAR-PEI

It looks like a miniature hippopotamus with badly fitting panty hose all over.
■ ROGER CARAS,
A CELEBRATION OF DOGS

MONDO CANINE

SHETLAND SHEEPDOG

A whole pack of wild dogs will scarcely ever venture to attack a flock of sheep guarded by even one of these faithful sheepdogs. . . . It ranks the sheep as its fellow brethren and thus gains confidence; and the wild dogs, though knowing that individual sheep are good to eat, yet partly consent to this view when seeing them in a flock with a shepherd-dog at their head.
■ CHARLES DARWIN

STAFFORDSHIRE BULL TERRIER

My father once owned a Staffordshire bull terrier which used to hang from a springy tree for anything up to five minutes at a time with its eyes shut in complete bliss.
■ GERALD L. WOOD

63

ST. BERNARD

The famed brandy cask is a myth. It probably began due to the fact that the lost traveler, once found, was usually offered brandy by the [Augustinian] Brother who accompanied the search dog. But the Brother carried the brandy, not the dog.
■ THE MONKS OF NEW SKETE,
HOW TO BE YOUR DOG'S BEST FRIEND

THE RIGHT PUP

If . . . you want a personal contact, if you are a lonely person and want, like Byron, "to know there is an eye will mark your coming and look brighter when you come," then choose a dog. Do not think it is cruel to keep a dog in a town flat. His happiness depends largely upon how much time you can spend with him and upon how often he may accompany you on an errand. He does not mind waiting for hours at your study door if he is finally rewarded by a ten minutes' walk at your side. Personal friendship means everything to a dog; but remember, it entails no small responsibility, for a dog is not a servant to whom you can easily give notice. And remember, too, if you are an over-sensitive person, that the life of your friend is much shorter than your own and a sad parting, after ten or fifteen years, is inevitable.

■ KONRAD LORENZ,
KING SOLOMON'S RING

Picking a puppy is, of course, a gamble and you treat it as such. In the same way a Las Vegas dice player might let a lady throw for him, I used to let my daughters pick out a puppy from the litters that we bred. Whereas I might be stuffy about the whole thing and fool with conformation, aggressiveness, and the like, the girls had a much better way of perceiving some aura about the dog that suited them. It was a mysterious rite, and I often, but quietly, disagreed with them; however, their instincts always proved sounder than my shallow knowledge.

■ GENE HILL,
"DOG DAZE"

You can recognize an alpha female puppy by her herding instinct; she will be alert as she pushes and herds the other puppies around, just

64

like a mother. As a rule, the female puppy does not vie to be the pack
leader.
■ DR. JANET RUCKERT,
ARE YOU MY DOG?

A bitch is more faithful than a dog, the intricacies of her mind are finer,
richer and more complex than his, and her intelligence is generally
greater. I have known very many dogs and can say with firm conviction
that of all creatures the one nearest to man, in the fineness of its
perceptions and its capacity to render true friendship, is a bitch. Strange
that in English her name has become a term of abuse.
■ KONRAD LORENZ,
MAN MEETS DOG

People like to go through the ritual of playing with a litter because
they feel that at least they are doing something to help in making the
choice. The prospective buyer sits in the middle of the litter and plays
with all the pups. The one that pulls at his cuff, pounces through the
pack, climbs up into his lap, and paws at his shirt to give him a love
lick is usually the one that wins his heart and gets bed and board for
life. Unfortunately, after the system of buying a dog by mail order,
this method of choosing could be your biggest error. By taking the pup
that shoves his way through the crowd to give you that face lick, most
likely you have picked the dominant dog in the litter, the bullheaded
one . . . the toughest to train.
■ RICHARD A. WOLTERS,
GAME DOG

65

THE CANINE

CONDITION

I realized clearly, perhaps for the first time, what strained and anxious lives dogs must lead, so emotionally involved in the world of men, whose affections they strive endlessly to secure, whose authority they are expected unquestioningly to obey, and whose mind they never can do more than imperfectly reach and comprehend. Stupidly loved, stupidly hated, acquired without thought, reared and ruled without understanding, passed on or "put to sleep" without care, did they, I wondered, these descendants of the creatures who, thousands of years ago in the primeval forests, laid siege to the heart of man, took him under their protection, tried to tame him, and failed—did they suffer from headaches?
■ J.R. ACKERLEY,
MY DOG TULIP

The poor dog, in life the firmest friend,
The first to welcome, foremost to defend,
Whose honest heart is still his master's own,
Who labours, fights, lives, breathes for him alone,
Unhonour'd falls, unnoticed all his worth,
Denied in heaven the soul he held on earth.
While man, vain insect! hopes to be forgiven,
And claims himself a sole exclusive heaven.
■ LORD BYRON,
INSCRIPTION ON THE MONUMENT OF A
NEWFOUNDLAND DOG

What kind of life a dog, even a big dog, acquires, I have sometimes tried to imagine by kneeling or lying full length on the ground and looking up. The world then becomes strangely incomplete: one sees little but legs. ■ E.V. LUCAS

A doctor I once knew told me of a spaniel he had taken to the North Country for the hunting. The dog had an encounter with a porcupine and returned to camp, his face bristling with quills. The pulling out of them had been a terribly painful business. He was laid on a table for the purpose. When the spaniel reached the limit of his endurance, he would catch his master's hand in his teeth, with a growl of warning, and he would be put on the floor for a breathing space. The dog would walk up and down whimpering in pain, but each time he returned to the table, raising his paws to be lifted again. This was repeated until all the quills were extracted.

■ MAZO DE LA ROCHE,
PORTRAIT OF A DOG

The dog is a religious animal. In his savage state he worships the moon and the lights that float upon the waters. These are his gods, to whom he appeals at night with long-drawn howls. In the domesticated state he seeks by his caresses to conciliate those powerful genii who dispense the good things of this world—to wit, men. He worships and honors men by the accomplishment of the rites passed down to him by his ancestors; he licks their hands, jumps against their legs, and when they show signs of anger towards him he approaches them crawling on his belly as a sign of humility, to appease their wrath.

■ ANATOLE FRANCE,
"THE COMING OF RIQUET"

I invoke the familiar muse, the city muse, the lively muse, so that she will help me sing of good dogs, pitiful dogs, muddied dogs, those

MONDO
CANINE

everyone shuns as stricken with plague and vermin, except the pauper whose colleagues they are, and the poet, who considers them with a fraternal eye. . . .

I sing of catastrophic dogs, of those who wander, alone, in the sinuous ravines of huge cities, and of those who tell abandoned people, with winks and witty eyes, "Take me along, and out of our two miseries perhaps we'll create a kind of happiness!"

"*Where do dogs go?*" once wrote Nestor Roqueplan in an immortal story he has probably forgotten. . . . Where do dogs go? You ask, you unmindful people. They go about their business.

Business meetings, love meetings. Through fog, through snow, through mud, during biting dog-days, in streaming rain, they go, they come, they trot, they slip under carriages, urged on by fleas, passion, need, or duty. Like us, they get up early in the morning, and they seek their livelihood or pursue their pleasures.

■ CHARLES BAUDELAIRE,
"*THE PARISIAN PROWLER*"

69

M A N ' S   I N H U M A N I T Y

T O   D O G

Dog may be Man's best friend, but Man is often Dog's severest critic, in spite of his historic protestations of affection and admiration. He calls an unattractive girl a dog, he talks acidly of dogs in the manger, he describes a hard way of life as a dog's life, he observes, cloudily, that this misfortune or that shouldn't happen to a dog, as if most slings and arrows should, and he describes anybody he can't stand as a dirty dog. He notoriously takes the names of the female dog and her male offspring in vain, to denounce blackly members of his own race. In all

Living on the edge of a Colorado wilderness, we learn of a distressing number of dumped dogs, abandoned by owners too lazy or unconcerned to take the trouble to find good homes for their disposable pets. These owners delude themselves into believing that, if dumped on the edge of the wilderness, their dogs will be able to take care of themselves. They will harken to the call of the wild. This notion is just plain idiotic.

What normally happens to dogs abandoned away from civ-

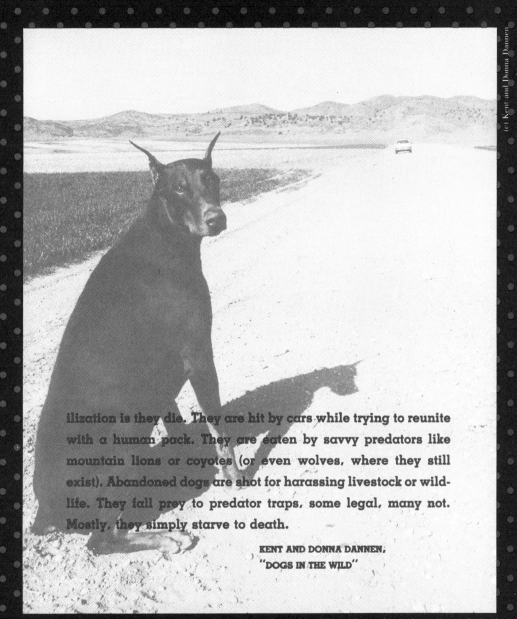

ilization is they die. They are hit by cars while trying to reunite with a human pack. They are eaten by savvy predators like mountain lions or coyotes (or even wolves, where they still exist). Abandoned dogs are shot for harassing livestock or wildlife. They fall prey to predator traps, some legal, many not. Mostly, they simply starve to death.

KENT AND DONNA DANNEN,
"DOGS IN THE WILD"

this disdain and contempt there is a curious streak of envy, akin to what the psychiatrists know as sibling jealousy. Man is troubled by what might be called the Dog Wish, a strange and involved compulsion to be as happy and carefree as a dog. . . .

■ JAMES THURBER,
"AND SO TO MEDVE"

After a particularly fierce blow he crawled to his feet, too dazed to rush. He staggered limply about, the blood flowing from nose and mouth and ears, his beautiful coat sprayed and flecked with bloody slaver. Then the man advanced and deliberately dealt him a frightful blow on the nose. All the pain he had endured was as nothing compared with the exquisite agony of this. With a roar that was almost lion-like in its ferocity, he again hurled himself at the man. But the man, shifting the club from right to left, coolly caught him by the under jaw, at the same time wrenching downward and backward. Buck described a complete circle in the air, and half of another, then crashed to the ground on his head and chest. For the last time he rushed. The man struck the shrewd blow he had purposely withheld for so long, and Buck crumbled up and went down, knocked utterly senseless.

■ JACK LONDON,
THE CALL OF THE WILD

Stealing someone's pet and selling it for research, it's heartless and cruel, but it's happening all over the United States. It's estimated that as many as a million dogs are stolen every year in this country, many ending up in medical experiments.

■ STONE PHILLIPS
ON *"20/20"*

The dog was in a large pot over the fire, in the middle of the lodge, and immediately on our arrival was dished up in large wooden bowls,

72

one of which was handed to each. The flesh appears very glutinous, with something of the flavor and appearance of mutton. Feeling something move behind me, I looked round, and found that I had taken my seat among a litter of fat young puppies. Had I been nice in such matters, the prejudices of civilization might have interfered with my tranquility, but, fortunately, I am not of delicate nerves, and continued quietly to empty my platter.

■ JOHN C. FREMONT

Although the Romans were not particularly fond of dogs, they were fond of their possessions, and the house of every well-to-do Roman had a dog posted in its entrance hall. In August of each year, at the beginning of the "dog days," they sacrificed a number of dogs, possibly to be granted safety from rabies, very common then.

■ KATHLEEN SZASZ,
PETISHISM

When a man's best friend is his dog, that dog has a problem.

■ EDWARD ABBEY

SHOW DOGS

Even those varieties of the dog which have been bred into grotesque deformity by the dog-fanciers are in good faith accounted beautiful by many. These varieties of dogs . . . are rated and graded in aesthetic value somewhat in proportion to the degree of grotesqueness and instability of the particular fashion which deformity takes in a given case. . . . This differential utility on the ground of grotesqueness and instability of structure is reducible to terms of a greater scarcity and consequent expense. The commercial value of canine monstrosities, such as the prevailing style of pet dogs both for men's and women's use, rests on their high cost of production, and their value to their owners lies chiefly in their utility as items of conspicuous consumption. Indirectly, through reflection upon their honorific expensiveness, a social worth is imputed to them; and so, by an easy substitution of words and ideas, they come to be admired and reputed beautiful.

■ THORSTEIN VEBLEN

The American Kennel Club disdains any dog without "papers" attesting that it is "purebred," even though the AKC exercises little or no control over the issuance of such papers. The result is that their mere possession is no guarantee of a dog's physical or mental soundness. Thus, being "purebred" has become a meaningless distinction. Many purebred dogs are purely awful. ■ HOWARD OGDEN

There are dogs you've never seen before back here, [at the Westminster Dog Show] there are dogs you've never heard of before. And there is a certain snootiness; Pomeranians speak only to poodles, and poodles only to God. ■ CHARLES KURALT
ON "48 HOURS"

MONDO
CANINE

UPI/Bettmann Newsphotos

SHOW DOGS:
A PERSONAL NOTE

I'm sorry, but I don't like show dogs. I don't like the fussy haircuts, the stuck-up parading around the ring, the bribe training. There's something deeply disturbing about animals who can look haughty and wretched at the same time. I don't like to watch them being groped by some twit in a tuxedo, and I don't like those silly names ("Champion Cabaret's Manuscript," "Champion Masquerade Par-T At Su-Gran," "Champion Luftnaus Abelarm Bee's Knees"). Even the announcers' descriptions sound like wine-talk, or art-speak, or any jargon employed by the cognoscenti to exclude the uninitiated. Show dogs are to real dogs what beauty contestants are to real women: too good to be true—too pretty to do anything but just stand there and look pretty.

I'm not crazy about show dog *people*, either. Many of them are arrogant, self-styled purists who judge dogs for their appearance while ignoring matters of soundness and function and spirit. They consider it their mission to "improve" the breeds, and they perform it autocratically and with disastrous results: their stewardship has produced a race of pampered canine inbeciles.

Show dogs are the antithesis of the open, genuine canine spirit. They're un-doglike.   ■ J.W.

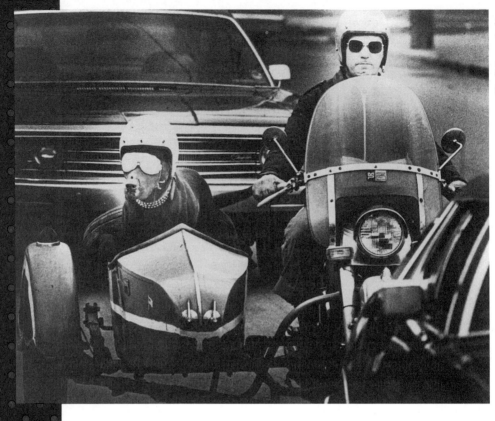

" A D V E N T U R E   D O G "

D A V E   B A R R Y

 I have this idea for a new television series. It would be a realistic action

show, patterned after the true-life experiences of my dog, Earnest. The name of the show would be "Adventure Dog."

The theme song would go:

> Adventure dog,
> Adventure doooooooggg
> Kinda big, kinda strong
> Stupid as a log.

Each episode would be about an exciting true adventure that happened to Earnest. For example, here's the script for an episode entitled: "Adventure Dog Wakes Up and Goes Outside":

It is 6:17 A.M. Adventure Dog is sleeping in the hall. Suddenly she hears a sound. Her head snaps up. Somebody is up! Time to swing into action!

Adventure Dog races down the hall and, skidding on all four paws, turns into the bathroom, where, to her total shock, she finds: The Master! Whom she has not seen since LAST NIGHT! YAYYYYYY!!

ADVENTURE DOG: Bark!

MASTER: DOWN, dammit!

Now Adventure Dog bounds to the front door, in case the Master is going to take her outside. It is a slim chance. He has only taken her outside for the past 2,637 consecutive mornings. But just in case, Adventure Dog is ready.

ADVENTURE DOG: Bark!

Can it be? Yes! This is unbelievable! The Master is coming to the door! Looks like Adventure Dog is going outside! YAAAYYY!

MASTER: DOWN, dammit!

Now the master has opened the door approximately one inch. Adventure Dog realizes that, at this rate, it may take the Master a full three-tenths of a second to open the door all the way. This is bad. He needs help. Adventure Dog alertly puts her nose in the crack and applies 600,000 pounds of force to the door.

MASTER: HEY!

DOOR: WHAM!

And now Adventure Dog is through the door, looking left, looking right, her finely honed senses absorbing every detail of the environment, every nuance and subtlety, looking for . . . Holy Smoke! There it is! The YARD! Right in the exact same place it was yesterday! This is turning out to be an UNBELIEVABLE adventure!

ADVENTURE DOG: Bark!

Adventure Dog is vaguely troubled. Some primitive version of a thought is rattling around inside her tiny cranium, like a BB in a tuna fish can. For she senses that there is some reason why the Master has let her outside. There is something he wants Adventure Dog to do. But what

MONDO CANINE

on Earth could it be? Before Adventure Dog can think of an answer, she detects . . . is this possible? Yes! It's a SMELL! Yikes! Full Red Alert!

ADVENTURE DOG: Sniff sniff sniff.

MASTER: Come on, Earnest.

ADVENTURE DOG: Sniff sniff sniff sniff sniff sniff sniff sniff.

No question about it. The evidence is clear. This is a smell, all right. And what's more, it's the smell of—this is so incredible—DOG WEEWEE! Right here in the yard!

MASTER: EARNEST!

ADVENTURE DOG: Sniff sniff sniff sniff sniff.

Adventure Dog is getting the germ of an idea. At first it seems farfetched, but the more she thinks about it, the more she thinks, hey, why not! The idea is—get ready—Adventure Dog is going to MAKE WEEWEE! Right now! Outside! It's crazy, but it just might work!

MASTER: Good GIRL.

What was that? It was a sound! Definitely. A sound coming from over there. Yes! No question about it. This is unbelievable! It's the MASTER out here in the yard! YAAAYY!

MASTER: DOWN, dammit!

THEME SONG SINGER: Adventure Dog, Adventure Dooooooggg . . .

ADVENTURE DOG: BARK!

MASTER: DOWN!

Bear in mind that this is only one episode. There are many other possiblities: "Adventure Dog Gets Fed," "Adventure Dog Goes for a Ride in the Car and Sees Another Dog and Barks Real Loud for the Next 116 Miles," etc. It would be the kind of family-oriented show your kids could watch, because there would be extremely little sex, thanks to an earlier episode, "Adventure Dog Has an Operation."

MONDO CANINE

DOG TRAINING

A dog likes to obey. It gives them security.

■ JAMES HERRIOT

Intelligent dogs rarely want to please people whom they do not respect.

■ W.R. KOEHLER,
THE KOEHLER METHOD OF DOG TRAINING

Don't make the mistake of treating your dogs like humans, or they'll treat you like dogs. ■ MARTHA SCOTT

Want to know how to train a dog in one sentence? It's simple. *Don't give commands you can't enforce.*

■ JEROME B. ROBINSON

When you point out something to a dog, he looks at your finger.

■ J. BRYAN, III,
HODGEPODGE TWO

If a dog will not come to you after he has looked you in the face, you ought to go home and examine your conscience.

■ WOODROW WILSON

The old saw about old dogs and new tricks only applies to certain people. ■ DANIEL PINKWATER,
"TRAIN YOUR DOG, DAMMIT!"

I don't train with fear, I just train the dogs to respect and trust me, and I teach them that I trust them and need them.

■ SUSAN BUTCHER

MONDO
CANINE

A really companionable and indispensable dog is an accident of nature. You can't get it by breeding for it, and you can't buy it with money. It just happens along. ■ E.B. WHITE,
"THE CARE AND TRAINING OF A DOG"

Teaching an animal to do tricks for home entertainment or commercial purposes I find demeaning and exploitative. Even the most simple tricks such as barking for food, rolling over on command, or raising a paw to shake hands are based upon subordinating the animal. For instance, paw raising and rolling over in dogs are part of the animals' natural submissive "body language" repertoire. Making animals perform such acts means making them display their submission, which, in gratifying the human ego, says much about our need to feel superior and in control. ■ DR. MICHAEL W. FOX

I do not believe in paying off a dog by shoving food into his mouth every time he does something he was bred to do. I like to think that the training is taking place in the head, not the stomach. A kind word in his ear is making the brain work, food in the stomach only makes the bowels work. ■ RICHARD A. WOLTERS,
GUN DOG

Few owners realize that the training of dogs, if done conscientiously, is quite a dangerous occupation and if a trainer is bitten badly many times, he could suffer a loss of confidence in his ability, which could be fatal to his work. ■ BARBARA WOODHOUSE,
NO BAD DOGS

We are to listen to a dog until we discover what is needed instead of imposing ourselves in the name of training.
■ THE MONKS OF NEW SKETE,
HOW TO BE YOUR DOG'S BEST FRIEND

When training a dog, it is important to leave it wanting to do more. In other words, train your dog until it is tired; you want your dog to *want* to work, not to *have* to work. Five to ten minutes of good work is worth its weight in performance. One handler mistake is trying to get the upper hand with the dog. The dog needs a sense of self-confidence, and it acquires this when the trainer shows it respect, so both dog and handler trust each other. There must be a true human-dog partnership.

■ DR. JANET RUCKERT,
ARE YOU MY DOG?

First you learn a new language, profanity; and second you learn not to discipline your dogs when you're mad, and that's most of the time when you're training dogs.

■ LOU SHULTZ,
1991 365 DOGS CALENDAR

It is quite wrong to attempt to instill obedience into a dog by punishment and equally senseless to beat him afterwards when, enticed by the scent of some game, he has run away during a walk. The beating will cure him not of running away, which lies farther back in his memory, but probably of the coming back, with which he will assuredly connect the punishment. The only way of curing such a deserter is to shoot something at him with a catapult just as he is preparing to make off. The shot must take the dog quite by surprise and it is better that he should not notice that this bolt from the blue was directed by the hand of his own master. The complete defenselessness of the animal against this sudden pain will make it all the more memorable for him, and this method has the additional advantage that it will not make him hand-shy.

■ KONRAD LORENZ,
MAN MEETS DOG

MONDO
CANINE

I cannot impress on my readers too strongly the necessity to be firm but kind to a puppy. His idea of your authority is forming, and if he knows you give in on the slightest whimper, you are whacked for life.

■ BARBARA WOODHOUSE,
DOG TRAINING MY WAY

A young pup should be disciplined by simply grabbing with one hand the scruff of the neck and giving it a good shake. This method approximates the technique a mother of a litter uses to keep order in a litter, to stop fighting between litter members, or to help wean her pups away from her to solid food. Discipline methods that reflect instinctual canine behavior will communicate displeasure in ways a dog can understand. Other corrections like throwing or hitting the dog with objects, spanking with newspapers, or simple pleading only serve human, not canine, ends, and do not communicate displeasure clearly to the dog.

■ THE MONKS OF NEW SKETE,
HOW TO BE YOUR DOG'S BEST FRIEND

83

Some suggest the rolled newspaper. In my opinion this is very cruel. It's wrong to teach a dog to fear a loud noise. A dog can be conditioned this way, become noise-shy and end up a nervous wreck. Reprimand has to be given immediately, not after the act when you've found wherever you've left your rolled-up newspaper. Also, is it any wonder why paperboys and postmen delivering papers get the seats of their pants taken out?

■ RICHARD A. WOLTERS,
HOME DOG

You do not have to strike your dog for doing wrong. Your frowns, finger shakes, and sharp words are enough. You do not have to reward

MONDO
CANINE

your dog with food. Your praise is its laurel. It wants to do what you
wish it to do. . . .
■ JEAN CRAIGHEAD GEORGE,
HOW TO TALK TO YOUR DOG

When I work a puppy or a young dog, I go by the positive method. I
use very little coercion, seldom scold or shout. Instead I praise heavily
when things are done right. When a dog is pleased at having learned
something, so am I, and when a lesson goes sour, I return, for a little
while, to the things that the dog *can* do, to keep her confidence up. If
a training session seems like it isn't going anywhere at all, I've learned
to stop everything and rethink it myself to find out if there is another
way to get the idea across to the dog.
■ GENE HILL,
"DAISY"

The best way to house-train a newly acquired young dog of about three
months is to watch him constantly during his first few hours in your house
and to interrupt him the moment he seems likely to deposit a *corpus
delicti* of either liquid or solid consistency. Carry him as quickly as
possible outside and set him down, always in the same place. When
he has done what is required of him, praise and caress him as though
he had performed a positive act of heroism. A puppy treated like this
very soon learns what is meant, and if he is taken out regularly, there
will soon be nothing more to clean up.
■ KONRAD LORENZ,
MAN MEETS DOG

Like any close relation between two people, there will be an occasional
clash of intents if not of wills, and you must work this out without loss
of intimacy.
■ GEORGE BIRD EVANS,
TROUBLES WITH BIRD DOGS

MONDO
CANINE

Never repeat a command. Most dogs are not deaf; they just choose not to listen. . . . Avoid a harsh tone and never yell. When you get inside your dog's head, you will realize that the dog is manipulative. If the dog knows it has the power to make you angry, it will love to control that. To keep its respect, be calm and firm.

■ CONNIE JANKOWSKI
WITH LAURIE RUBENFELD,
"PUPPY TRAINING SECRETS"

In praising dogs I always use the words "What a good dog." I have lined a class of dogs up and told the owners to praise them in their usual manner, then told them to prefix the phrase with the word "what." The effect on the dogs is undeniable. For some extraordinary reason the word "what" electrifies them and gives them so much more pleasure than ordinary praise. After telling listeners to a broadcast to say this to their dogs, I had dozens of letters saying it really does work.

■ BARBARA WOODHOUSE,
NO BAD DOGS

85

The training of the dog is something which should be left to the boy, as this teaches him responsibility and accustoms him to the use of authority, probably the only time he will ever have a chance to use it. If, for example, the dog insists on following the boy when he is leaving the house, even after repeated commands to "Go back on home!" the boy must decide on one of two courses. He must either take the dog back to the house and lock it in the cellar, or, as an alternative course, he can give up the idea of going out himself and stay with the dog. The latter is the better way, especially if the dog is in good voice and given to screaming the house down.

■ ROBERT BENCHLEY,
"YOUR BOY AND HIS DOG"

MONDO
CANINE

Chasing cars . . . can be corrected by using two assistants . . . [and some tin cans attached to a wire] to produce three surprises. Use a car the dog doesn't know. You, the trainer, hide in the car so the dog doesn't see you. One assistant drives the car past your home and Towser, the neighborhood daredevil, charges. The other assistant hits him with the cans for surprise number one. Stop the car. Just to make sure that he's learned his lesson, you jump out of the car making a lot of noise. This will be the second surprise—he never expected to see you. Giving him a good licking—that's the third. Send him home, shaken but cured.

■ RICHARD A. WOLTERS,
FAMILY DOG

If you have an older dog that is reluctant to swim, it probably had a bad experience around water. Somebody tried to push, pull, or throw it in, and in the process made the dog water-shy.

If a dog truly has a fear of water, there is little you can do to reassure it. The dog must overcome the fear itself. One method guaranteed to make a voluntary swimmer out of any dog is as follows:

On a warm day put the dog on a small raft anchored a few yards from shore. Don't say anything—just leave it there. Then go ashore and, in plain sight of the marooned dog, begin playing with another dog or throwing a ball back and forth with another person. Pay no attention to the dog whatsoever. The dog will cry and whine, but eventually its desire to join you will overcome its fear of water and it will voluntarily swim ashore.

Repeat this regularly, and gradually move the raft farther from shore, increasing the distance the dog must swim. Because it made up its own mind to enter the water and found that it could swim, the dog will overcome its fear.

■ JEROME B. ROBINSON,
"FEAR OF SWIMMING"

When we train dogs for police work we teach them not to be skittish around firearms. We'll send the dog after a simulated bad guy and he'll turn and shoot blanks right at the dog. We keep doing it until they learn to ignore the loud bang and the smoke, and after a while it really doesn't phase them. Unfortunately it also gives them a false sense of security, and sometimes that costs them their lives.

■ OFFICER RICK MIGLIA,
MONROVIA, CALIFORNIA,
POLICE DEPARTMENT

When a doting person gets down on all fours and plays with his dog's rubber mouse, it only confuses the puppy and gives him a sense of insecurity. He gets the impression that the world is unstable and wonders whether he is supposed to walk on his hind legs and learn to smoke cigars.   ■ COREY FORD

87

Labradors have the gentlest, sweetest dispositions of any breed. I have had Junie, Dinah, Mr. Tambo, Missy, "the Labradorable Sassy," and Dixie. Dixie's manners would have been perfect, but for one fault: when she was left alone in the car, she would chew on the armrests. We finally found a simple way to break her, and I commend it to all of you with a similar problem. Ask your friendly neighborhood pharmacist for a one-ounce bottle of thumb-sucking cure such as THUM. Paint it on the armrests, or on anything else your dog finds appetizing, and we guarantee that his next nibble will cure him.

■ J. BRYAN, III,
HODGEPODGE TWO

Huckleberry rests his head on the arm of my chair and gazes till I look up from work to say (not very sternly) "now cut that out." He does. Instead he wriggles his muzzle under my elbow and lets me know that an ear-rub would be welcome. I rub with my right hand and type with my left. Huck nibbles at a flea suspect that turns out to be the button on my sleeve. Then he runs to the vestibule and brings me a boot, for which I pat him on the head. I do not want the boot, but it is what he thinks I want, so I want him to think that I want it. I am training him to fetch. This is how I encourage him.

■ DATUS C. PROPER,
PHEASANTS OF THE MIND

A couple years ago, a dairyman in Virginia's Shenandoah Valley had a fine young Border Collie, keen as blazes. Since the young dog was often underfoot, the dairyman trained the dog to "Stay!" so he could go about his chores unhampered. Twice a day he'd send the dog for his cows, and after the cows were in the milking parlor he'd point at a patch of cool shade: "Lie down. Stay! You *stay!*" One hot August afternoon, the dairyman was working his Holsteins, routine worming, through his cattle chutes. When he shooed his cows out of the pens they came out fast and hard, right over the dog, who never budged from where he was told to STAY. The dog was killed, the dairyman was overcome with remorse. He'd never, he vowed, train a dog so well again.

■ DONALD McCAIG,
EMINENT DOGS, DANGEROUS MEN

It is almost but not quite possible to turn a dog into a robot. Precision in a dog's work no more destroys his personality than it destroys a dancer's grace, no more than cell structure destroys the suppleness of a leaf or a dog, and dog training is an art, not a social occasion, you have to mean everything you say and there are no compromises.

■ VICKI HEARNE,
THE WHITE GERMAN SHEPHERD

MONDO
CANINE

I own two dogs, and they both have been trained to respond immediately to my voice. For example, when we're outside, all I have to do is issue the following standard dog command: "Here Earnest! Here Zippy! C'mon! Here! I said come HERE! You dogs COME HERE RIGHT NOW! ARE YOU DOGS LISTENING TO ME? HEY!!!" And instantly both dogs, in unison, like a precision drill team, will continue trotting in random directions, sniffing the ground.

■ DAVE BARRY,
"YELLOW JOURNALISM"

89

A CONVERSATION

WITH

VICKI HEARNE

JW: *First off I'd like to know your opinion of Konrad Lorenz's work on dogs, the idea that domestication began with jackals and wolves forming two strains of canids, and the whole domination idea . . .*

VH: That stuff drives me up the wall. Every third client I talk to has this idea in their head, and it's phony as all hell. Not in the way he said it, but in the way it's working out, it's a bunch of bullshit.

JW: *Basically, what are we talking about?*

VH: Well, his idea—if I've got it right, and to be fair to him, I'm not sure I've got it right—was that animals, social animals, live in a hierarchy, and within that hierarchy there's this pack leader. So when you have domesticated dogs, cats, horses, whatever, you, the human, are the pack leader. It's bullshit. It's good bullshit, it's really good, but it doesn't work out in real life. In real life the dog says, "You're cute, but I've got things to do."

JW: *Depending somewhat on the dog's personality, right?*

VH: Well, yes, being scientific here, yes.

JW: *Are some dogs more submissive than others?*

Vicki Hearne is the author of Adam's Task: Calling Animals by Name *and* Bandit: Dossier of a Dangerous Dog. *She is a lecturer in creative writing at Yale and a professional dog and horse trainer.*

VH: Yes, but—it's not Konrad Lorenz's fault—but the idea of dominance/ submission is the biggest superstition of this century.

JW: *Really?*

VH: Really.

JW: *Talk about exploding a myth . . .*

VH: Well, I'm sorry.

JW: *It's just that everybody loves the idea that we humans are naturally superior . . .*

VH: That we're natural leaders . . .

JW: *Right, and that because we have many similar social habits, it would have been easy for the wolves to accept a human as a "pack leader."*

VH: Bullshit. Do you know what the problem is in training a wolf? They're too submissive. That's what messes you up every time. They're so timid, so submissive, it's really hard to work with them. We're all going to have to give up our religious ideas, because wolves don't work that way, because dogs don't work that way.

JW: *All right then, speaking of religious ideas, in* Adam's Task *you make the point that anthropomorphism is not always wrong, it's just misapplied.*

VH: When I was writing that book anthropomorphism was the big sin. Nowadays, there are people who are making a lot of money out of being *for* anthropomorphism, and I have had occasion to refuse the position of High Priestess of Anthropomorphism. But I don't see any more reason that you shouldn't infer from yourself to your dog than from yourself to your wife or your husband. My husband comes home, and he's tired and he droops. And my dog droops sometimes. Now why shouldn't I say he's "tired"? Husband, dog, whatever.

JW: *But being tired is not necessarily that hard to accept as an animal quality or condition. What about heroism? What about when a dog chews through plywood to get into a burning house in order to save a member of his human family?*

91

VH: Well, it's just like with people. It's heroism. I know a bull terrier who was the lead in a film in which just that happened. Fire, dog goes in. Now his owner has to put screens around her fireplace because he wants to go in and do *that*! [Laughs].

JW: *He wants to go in and save the logs from the fire?*

VH: Well, whatever it is he wants to do, he wants to go in there and do it.

JW: *Can we say they act with courage, nobility?*

VH: Oh, you bet.

JW: *Self-sacrifice?*

VH: You can quote me on that. They do. It drives me nuts, really. Dogs are so good, and I am so inadequate, that it drives me nuts.

JW: *You write about a dog named Belle who's modeled on Annie, your own dog.*

VH: She's in my lap right now.

JW: *Does she give any indication that she knows we're talking about her?*

VH: No, she's bored.

JW: *So, they're not so anthropomorphic that they have subscriptions to, say, TLS?*

VH: Dogs can't read or write. That's really important to remember. People have no idea.

JW: *You say that Belle "has a lot of natural judgment and learns to distinguish between idiots and real hoods." We normally consider judgment a human quality. What is hers based on? Where does it come from?*

VH: Well, love. She hangs out. She learns.

JW: *The same way people learn, by experience and observation?*

VH: Right. And she has senses that enable her to make different kinds of observations than we can. She is, as all dogs are, *aware*. She is much more conscious than I am of the *right now*. There was a public relations film that Scotland Yard did. In the film there was an Irish wolfhound and a marksman who could drop a quarter, draw and shoot it before it hit the ground. They gave him the task: hit the dog with blanks. That's all, just hit the dog. And he couldn't, because the dog knew before he knew when he was going to draw. Another story: policeman training film. Policeman stops woman, she lifts her shirt with her left hand; with her right hand she pulls a gun and shoots him. In the version of this with the dog, she doesn't get to do that, because the dog knows.

JW: *How?*

VH: The dog is paying attention. The dog is not distracted by the girl lifting her shirt, which is symbolic for seduction. So, now you're going to ask, "What is it that they are not distracted by?" Right?

JW: *Well, the extraneous?*

VH: Except that the extraneous is everything that civilization means.

JW: *Which is your point, isn't it, when you say, "They're paying attention"? We're distracted and they're paying attention.*

VH: And they drive me nuts. I had a client who was taking lessons in how to work a dog and he said, "Oh, it's so wonderful the way they read your mind," and I said, "It's not wonderful, it's horrible." When you hang out with dogs in this way, the trouble is that if they read your mind and find nothing there, they do nothing. Or if they read your mind and find junk there, which is the usual situation, they do junk.

JW: *They seem to know what you're thinking or feeling before you know. There's even a dog who lives with an epileptic, who predicts her seizures by as much as half an hour. They have a lot to tell us if only we'd pay attention.*

VH: Except that nobody wants to pay attention. I mean, nobody wants to bother to learn how to talk to the dog to find out about what's going

93

to happen half an hour from now. We're too busy.

JW: *You write about people who are "natural bitees." Are they extreme examples of having junk in your head?*

VH: That was a somewhat unfriendly sentence, but yes.

JW: *But aren't there also dogs who are known as "biters"?*

VH: Yes, but they're so rare. I've spent four years scrutinizing biting incident tapes for the Center for Disease Control, and by and large, dogs get it right and then move out of the way.

JW: *Mail carriers say that cocker spaniels are the biggest biters and the worst curs.*

VH: Cocker spaniels are an enormously popular breed, and when a breed is popular, the breeder has no incentive to watch for and stop temperament problems. So you get a lot of cockers and miniature poodles that are really quite sharp, to put it mildly.

JW: *Has the American Kennel Club done a disservice by promoting the breeding of dogs for appearance to the exclusion of physical and mental soundness?*

VH: The problem is, look at what you'd have to do to breed dogs to *anti-*AKC standards. You would have to go hunt or be a policeman. Think about how many people would be willing to follow their dog into the woods, say if there were a woods.

JW: *Are you saying we get the dogs we deserve?*

VH: No, unfortunately, or fortunately, we get better than we deserve. No, I would love to join the attack on the AKC, but the AKC isn't the problem, though the fact that it is not the Vatican is a point which many of its members fail to observe. The problem is human intelligence.

JW: *The AKC's problem is that it draws its membership from the human race?*

VH: The AKC's problem is, it is stupid. The AKC is flawlessly stupid, as most people are. But the AKC runs obedience trials. They're corrupt,

MONDO
CANINE

they're seriously corrupt, but where else can you find obedience trials? Give them credit for that much.

JW: *The only game in town?*

VH: Right.

JW: *What about the pit bull problem?*

VH: What problem?

JW: *If we believe the reports in the press and on television, pit bulls are a monstrous breed . . .*

VH: Well, turn off your goddam television. I actually have another existence—as a scholarly person—and I have been doing, over the past four years, very scholarly, heavy-duty work about dog-bite-associated fatalities. Do you want to know the most common cause of dog-bite-attack-related fatalities? Small boys. As near as I can figure out reading the data, small boys go up to a dog, they poke a finger in the dog's ear, nose, anus, whatever, and the dog growls or shakes his head. Now, in such a case a small *girl* says, "Oh, he doesn't like to be poked." But a small boy says, "Ah, there must be someplace *else* I can poke him!"

JW: *Have you found any data on the incidence of bites according to breed?*

VH: It's totally unreliable. I've looked, I've looked wholeheartedly, but I can't find it. There is no data.

JW: *Nothing to suggest that pit bulls are any more aggressive than miniature poodles?*

VH: Nothing. I swear to you, I would have loved it to turn out, say, that Malamutes are bad, but in fact, there's nothing.

JW: *What do you have against Malamutes?*

VH: Well, they're Nord nerds, see?

JW: *They're spacey?*

VH: Among other things.

JW: *Getting back to small boys, and children in general, in* Man Meets Dog *Lorenz talks about what he calls "the canine habit of chivalrous treatment of puppies, bitches and, particularly, the children of the master."*

VH: The truth is that dogs look around and say, "That kid's screwing up." Lorenz was good, but he didn't look at a couple of details, one of which is that the family dog often regards the family baby as a nuisance. Correctly. I, myself, am a mother. I know the situations in which you have "The Baby" and "The Doggie" and I assure you that my dogs knew that infant human beings leave heaven behind when the stork brings them. Nonetheless, most dogs are really good about babies. The proverbial baby on the blanket is not a myth. The dog goes out there, runs around, and guards—except if it's a Malamute. Dogs do try to tell you stuff. They try hard, but mostly people say, "Shut up, go away." With good reason, because dogs are a lot of trouble. So, normally, with the baby on the blanket, the dog is running around yelling his head off, with no apparent reason. There's rarely an obvious threat, a nice enemy or serpent or whatever. Stupid dog! So, in real life this becomes the form: the dog yells at you and you yell back, "Shut up, dog!"

JW: *Do dogs smile?*

VH: Yes, animals make little jokes. For example, I was jumping my Airedale the other day and he refused to jump and in his halt threw his head up and said, "Tyranny!" And I laughed, then I still made him jump.

JW: *You also wrote that he can appreciate a good joke . . .*

VH: Oh, yes, well, Airedales are just hopeless, really hopeless. We were working with dumbbells, and the Airedale influenced me to put the dumbbell on end. He thought it was so funny, and he jumped and threw the thing around—I hate Airedales, okay? Airedales . . . an Airedale will do an incredible display of nobility and then just with a little twist make it all fall down. That's what that blasted Airedale does. I don't want to discuss him.

JW: *But he did appreciate your bit of humor in placing the dumbbell differently.*

VH: Appreciated, enlarged on, and destroyed, okay?

JW: *He went too far?*

VH: I don't want to discuss Airedales.

JW: *All right, then, let's get back to the original question. Why do dogs smile? Are they imitating human behavior?*

VH: No, they smile because they're happy when they've done one over on us.

JW: *What, there's this friendly competition . . .*

VH: Friendly? I hate dogs, have I said that before? I hate dogs. They destroy me.

JW: *Tell me about your first dog.*

VH: That's not under the heading *I Hate Dogs*, that's under the heading *My Old Dog*. I was young, a baby, four or five, and the dog's name was Saint Stephen, I kid you not. He was a collie. He followed my bus to school and was there with me through this and that. He was so good. There was a point where my mother objected, you see, to this business of the dog going to school. The bus driver said, "Well, I can't stop him because if I close the door, he still gets the scent and follows." They ended up letting him ride the bus to school and attend class as well. So, you see, there was this bad dog. Everyone was upset, you understand, because this dog would not behave. He was *taught* to behave, but he didn't.

A neighbor woman was quite worried about her children being bitten by the dog. Saint Stephen was doing the proverbial herding dog's version of baby-on-the-blanket, which is to circle toddlers while they are playing, to keep them in the yard, and he bumped the woman's child. Maybe she thought that controlling the dog was the way to control her child. Perhaps she was fonder of the sauce than she should have been. I'm not sure—maybe I'm making it up. She asked the Air Police— we lived on an air base—to take the dog away. My parents stood firm and, in the end of it, that didn't happen. It did happen, however, that Saint Stephen died. Someone put ground glass in his food.

DOG LANGUAGE

BARKING

It is a . . . remarkable fact that the dog, since being domesticated, has learnt to bark in at least four or five distinct tones. Although barking is a new art, no doubt the wild parent-species of the dog expressed their feelings by cries of various kinds. With the domesticated dog we have the bark of eagerness, as in the chase; that of anger, as well as growling; the yelp or howl of despair, as when shut up; the baying at night; the bark of joy, as when starting on a walk with his master; and the very distinct one of demand or supplication, as when wishing for a door or window to be opened.

■ CHARLES DARWIN,
THE DESCENT OF MAN

Dogs have a lot to communicate to a person who's willing to listen. My dogs have five or six different howls: happy howls, sad howls, change-in-the-weather howls. Bitches in heat have incredibly flirtatious howls.

■ SUSAN BUTCHER

When the sounds of traffic die down and the last train has rumbled off to the city, Leon, a mutt at the bottom of the hill near the swamp, awakens and barks once. I hear him and wait. He barks again, then again; and he waits. Apparently he hears another voice that I cannot, for the next time Leon barks, he is excited. Finally I hear the distant dog, for someone has let him out. He barks, "Bow, bow, bow," for almost two minutes. A third dog speaks up, then far over the hill toward the next town a fourth sounds. The dogs are checking in, calling out their identities, letting each other know where they are, keeping tabs, keeping in touch—messages they can send only when the town has quieted down and all but the dogs and night animals are asleep. I find the night check-in reassuring. The dogs, by taking roll call, are saying, "All is well."

■ JEAN CRAIGHEAD GEORGE,
HOW TO TALK TO YOUR DOG

A P A   D O G

C O M M U N I C A T I O N   T A B L E

B Y   D O U G L A S   K I R K

This table, compiled from observations over the years by Animals of the Performing Arts, is a listing of the main "words" in what appears to be a universal dog language. By no means does this listing represent all of the thoughts, emotions and concepts that dogs communicate, but it does include many of the "words and phrases" most easily recognizable by dog owners. How many of these things can you recognize in your dog? What happens when you try expressing yourself to your dog using these sounds or actions? Does your dog look as if it understands what you are trying to say?

VERBAL COMMUNICATION

Verbalization	English Equivalent	Initiating Action
BARKS		
Rapid	"Danger! Intruder!"	Confrontation with stranger or unusual situation
Sudden	"Look out!" or "Look at this!"	Dog surprised or startled
Sharp Greeting	"Don't do that!"	Disciplining puppies
	"Hi, how are you?"	Welcoming return of friend
Play	"Let's play"	Desire to play
Incessant	"I'm lonely"	Confinement
Yelp	"Ouch!"	Sudden pain
GROWLING		
Soft	"Beware!"	Confrontation with strange person or dog
Growl leading to bark	"I'm prepared to defend!"	Confrontation with danger
Play (teeth hidden)	"I'm having fun!"	Usually during play
CRIES, WHIMPERS		
Lengthy whine	"I want"	Dog wants out, etc.
Whimpering cry	"That hurts" or "I'm scared"	At vet's or in other unusual situation
OTHER		
Bay	"Come here" or "Follow me"	Chasing prey
Howl	"I feel abandoned"	Confinement

NONVERBAL COMMUNICATION

EYES, EARS*

Direct stare	"I challenge you"	Confrontation
Avoiding eye contact	"I want to avoid a challenge"	Confrontation
Ears erect	"What's that?" or "I'm listening"	Interesting sound
Ears back, flat against head	"I'm afraid" or "I'm protecting myself"	Dog is challenged or in frightening situation
Ears relaxed	"I'm comfortable"	Surrounded by friends

TAIL*

Straight out	"I may attack"	Challenging intruder
Slight wag	"Hi"	Meeting friend
Big wag	"Wow—It's great to see you again!"	Meeting friend after separation
Down	"I'm not too sure about this"	Unknown situation
Tucked between legs	"I'm scared"	Threatened

POSTURE

Crouched, front legs extended	"Let's play!"	Playful mood
Body slightly lowered, feet braced	"I'm ready to fight."	Dog accepts challenge
Stiff-legged stance	"I dare you to fight"	Confrontation
Exposes underside	"I give up"	Submission
Scraping ground	"Everyone take note"	Usually after defecation
Urination	"This is mine"	Marking territory

* Cutting off a dog's ears or tail (cropping and docking) may seriously impair its ability to communicate with other dogs.

BODY LANGUAGE

But Vorace did not lie down. She snorted and stretched her paws which, for a dog, is the same as putting on a hat to go out. She went up to her master and her yellow eyes asked plainly: "Well?"

■ COLETTE,
"THE BITCH"

Presently he came, sinking his body lower as he advanced and at last crawling, and when he arrived at the shepherd's feet he turned himself over on his back—that eloquent action which a dog uses when humbling himself before and imploring mercy from one mightier than himself, man or dog.

■ W. H. HUDSON,
A SHEPHERD'S LIFE

103

Young dogs lie on their backs, all four feet in the air, when they meet an older stronger dog; they know who is boss and are showing the other dog so by giving the "pax" sign, which is exposing the tummy to an enemy.

■ BARBARA WOODHOUSE,
NO BAD DOGS

A dog that wants to be submissive and friendly will avoid eye-to-eye contact. His ears will be flattened against his head; his tail will be low and will wag slowly. Some dogs will roll over on their back to show submission, or they may crawl toward you on their belly. Unfortunately, some will piddle, which is an act acceptable in the dog world; others will lift a forepaw as if to shake hands. Many dogs will give a greeting grin much like a human smile.

■ RICHARD A. WOLTERS,
HOME DOG

Their tails are high and tongues awag—the twin banners of sled dog contentment.

■ CLARA GERMANI

The abdomen was grossly distended and I could read the tell-tale symptoms of pain: the catch in the respirations, the retracted commissures of the lips, the anxious, preoccupied expression of the eyes.

■ JAMES HERRIOT,
"HAVE A CIGAR"

Jaw tremors express intense emotion. My Airedale quivered her lower jaw when I brought another dog into the house, when she smelled a deer on the wind, when she heard a record of wolves howling, and when she looked upon a human infant.

■ JEAN CRAIGHEAD GEORGE,
HOW TO TALK TO YOUR DOG

104

TAIL WAGGING

Dogs laugh, but they laugh with their tails.

■ MAX EASTMAN

The old hound wags his shaggy tail,
And I know what he would say:
It's over the hills we'll bound old hound,
Over the hills and away. ■ GEORGE MEREDITH

Dogs wave tails or plumes, according to breed, in several indicative waves. There is wide sweep of expectancy, or the more vigorous movement of greeting. Or, tail under tummy, a subterranean waggle which can be pleasure tinged with guilt or fear.

■ ELMA WILLIAMS

I have rarely found a dog with a gaily carried tail, which curled over its back or sideways, of any value [for military purposes]. This method of carrying the tail seems to indicate a certain levity of character, quite at variance with the serious duties required.

■ COLONEL H.E. RICHARDSON,
BRITISH WAR DOGS

Some dogs are so shy that they will not, I will even say cannot, allow strangers to touch them. Such dogs frequently assume a cringing attitude, and therein lies the difficulty, for they often wag their tails deferentially. Only a knowledgeable observer will notice that the dog is trying to avoid the human touch, and crouches lower and lower beneath the hand which for some reason unknown to the animal is trying to stroke it. Should the tactlessly importunate human being persist in his attentions and actually touch the dog, the terrified animal may lose control of itself and snap like lightning and with punishing severity at the offending hand. A considerable number of dog bites are attributable to this kind of biting from fear. The victim of this surprise attack blames the dog all the more for having first of all wagged its tail.

■ KONRAD LORENZ,
MAN MEETS DOG

What a wonderful indicator of happiness is the dog's tail; the half-mast wag with the very tip of the tail, showing nervous expectation; the half-mast slow wag of the interested dog who wants to know what master is saying but doesn't quite pick it up; the full-mast wag of excitement and happiness when he is really happy; and last but not least, the tail between the legs of the nervous, shy or unhappy dog who trusts no one and to whom life is a burden.

■ BARBARA WOODHOUSE,
NO BAD DOGS

The dog wags it tail only at living things. A tail wag, the equivalent of a human smile, is bestowed upon people, dogs, cats, squirrels, even mice and butterflies—but no lifeless things. A dog won't wag its tail to its dinner or to a bed, car, stick, or even a bone.

■ JEAN CRAIGHEAD GEORGE,
HOW TO TALK TO YOUR DOG

SCENT COMMUNICATION

My father used to discuss what was afoot in the Potomac River bottomlands with his hound dog, Spike. He would tell him, "Hunt up a squirrel," and Spike would circle the forest until he picked up a squirrel scent. He would run the animal up a tree and announce it until Dad caught up. Spike found a raccoon when my father wanted a raccoon and deer when he wanted a deer. When they were simply out to investigate the forest and learn what was around, Spike would tell Dad what scent he had come upon. He had a different voice for each animal. A rabbit was a high yipe, a raccoon a series of sharp barks, a squirrel a low yip, and a deer—well, that was a rapidly fired succession of barks, yipes, and bellows, a dog's name for the quintessential odor.

■ JEAN CRAIGHEAD GEORGE,
HOW TO TALK TO YOUR DOG

One of the most obnoxious behaviors for many dog owners is that of the dog when it finds some foul-smelling material. Dogs love to roll in obnoxious organic material because they have a highly evolved sense of smell, probably a million times better than ours, and I believe that they have an esthetic sense in this modality: they like to wear odors much as we, a more visually oriented species, like to wear bright clothes or something different for a while. Wolves enjoy rolling in meat or some other food they particularly like before they actually eat it. This again may mean that "wearing" certain odors is an esthetic experience, the aroma remaining to be savored long after the meal has been eaten!

■ DR. MICHAEL W. FOX,
SUPERDOG

Dogs read the world through their noses and write their history in urine. Urine is another and highly complex source of social information; it is a language, a code, by means of which they not only express their feelings and emotions, but communicate with and appraise each other. Tulip is particularly instructive in this matter when she is in season, for on these occasions she has numerous callers who leave the marks of their attention round the front door. On her way in and out she reads, with her long black nose, these superimposed stains, and the care with which she studies them is so meticulous that she gives the impression of actually identifying her acquaintances and friends.

■ J.R. ACKERLEY,
MY DOG TULIP

Dogs need to sniff the ground; it's how they keep abreast of current events. The ground is a giant dog newspaper, containing all kinds of late-breaking dog news items, which, if they are especially urgent, are often continued in the next yard. We live next to an aircraft-carrier-sized dog named Bear who is constantly committing acts of prize-winning journalism around the neighborhood, and my dogs are major fans of his work. Each morning, while I am shouting commands at them, they race around and scrutinize the most recent installments of the ongoing Bear oeuvre, vibrating their bodies ecstatically to communicate their critical comments ("Bear has done it AGAIN!" "This is CLASSIC Bear!" etc.)

■ DAVE BARRY,
"YELLOW JOURNALISM"

MONDO CANINE

THE CANINE SMILE

As we came into the bank at Dawson, there sat Spot, waiting for us, his ears pricked up, his tail wagging, his mouth smiling, extending a hearty welcome to us.
■ JACK LONDON,
"THAT SPOT"

As we passed along on our tour of inspection, a smiling dog barked joyously and waved its tail at us from the top of every kennel.
■ COLONEL H.E. RICHARDSON,
BRITISH WAR DOGS

I lifted the pups out one by one and examined them. Susie didn't mind in the least but appeared to be smiling with modest pride as I handled her brood.
■ JAMES HERRIOT,
"A MOMENTOUS BIRTH"

At the words "go out," Vorace grinned and began to pant gently, showing her beautiful teeth and the fleshy petal of her tongue.
■ COLETTE,
"THE BITCH"

And what a smile of attentive obligingness, of incorruptible innocence, of affectionate submission, of boundless gratitude and total self-abandonment lit up, at the least caress, that adorable mask of ugliness! Whence exactly does that simple smile emanate? From the ingenuous and melting eyes? From the ears pricked up to catch the words of man? From the forehead that unwrinkled to appreciate and love, or from the stump of a tail that wriggled at the other end to testify to the intimate and impassioned joy that filled his small being, happy once more to encounter the hand or the glance of the god to whom he surrendered himself?

■ MAURICE MAETERLINCK,
"OUR FRIEND, THE DOG"

Christabel regards me as a comedian of sorts, and always knows when I am trying to be funny for her sake, and always smiles (there is no smile quite like a poodle's), and if the joke is a big production number, such as my opening the door to the downstairs lavatory when she asks to be let out, she gives her guttural laugh, turns her head slowly, and lets my wife in on the gag.

■ JAMES THURBER,
"CHRISTABEL: PART TWO"

109

BAD DOG!

Nobody's perfect, okay? Because of their close association with hu-

mans, dogs are sometimes prone to human frailties. And much of the behavior that we might term *canine* frailty only seems that way from our point of view: there's nothing inherently evil about barking, chewing, hole digging, and the most serious of all canine crimes, biting.

According to the Center for Disease Control in Atlanta, dog bite is a major public health problem in America, with over a million reported dog bites each year and probably several times that number going unreported, the majority of which consist of pets biting their owners. The American Medical Association estimates that each year over 40,000 children are bitten *in the face* by the family dog.

Frequently the victims claim that a previously trustworthy dog bit "without warning." But the fact is that a dog is not likely to attack without provocation and will in most cases give a warning or "bite cue" first. For example, in the case of "fear bites," dogs who are afraid of strangers or are hand-shy—and who will not bite if the human simply walks away and leaves them alone—usually give ample warning of their distress at being confronted: they growl, cower, and look frantically for a way out. Only if the human persists in trying to make physical contact will the dog bite in desperation.

And not all dog bites are equal. In many cases dogs restrain themselves when they bite; they pull their punches, as they have been bred to do.

Dogs will bite family members if they consider them (a) weaker than themselves (i.e., inferior "pack members") and (b) in need of discipline. These bites are almost always inhibited, single bites (unlike lethal, all-out, multiple-bite attacks). These disciplinary nips are the canine equivalent of a slap on the wrist. This explanation is of little consolation to the parents of an "inferior" family member who happens to be a defenseless toddler, and if the dog's behavior persists, there is no safe alternative to separating dog and child permanently.

Many bites result from misunderstandings or accidents. In one such incident, a large male dog killed a grandmother with one bite. It was reported in the press as a vicious, unprovoked attack, and the dog was immediately destroyed lest he kill again. Actually, the elderly woman tripped over the dog while he was sleeping, and he responded with a single disciplinary nip to show the weaker "pack member" that he would not tolerate being awakened in the night. Unfortunately for the woman (and the dog), the bite severed a main artery.

111

Injured dogs will often bite anyone who attempts to touch or move them, and severe injuries can result when a human tries to break up a dog fight. These distress or heat-of-battle bites can hardly be considered intentional and can be prevented with the use of caution on the part of humans.

It is unfortunate that dogs will occasionally bite for no reason, and in rare instances one or more dogs will viciously attack children and, even more rarely, adults. It is fortunate that only a tiny fraction of all dog bites occur during these uninhibited, all-out attacks, because they are often fatal.

Average number of mail carriers that are bitten by dogs each day: 9
■ *HARPER'S INDEX*

Let dogs delight to bark and bite
For God hath made them so.
■ ISAAC WATTS

A known psychopath, Bluey would attack himself if nothing else was available. He used to chase himself in circles trying to bite his own balls off. To avert instant death, I was supposed to call out from the front gate when I arrived and not open it until I was told that Bluey had been chained up. One day I opened it too early and Bluey met me on the front path. I don't know where he had come from—probably around the side of the house—but it was as if he had come up out of the ground on a lift. He was nasty enough when chained up but on the loose he was a bad dream. Barking from the stomach, he opened a mouth like a great wet tropical flower. When he snapped it shut, my right foot was inside it.

If Bluey hadn't been as old as the hills, my foot would have come right off. Luckily his teeth were in ruins, but even so I was a few tendons short of becoming an amputee. Since Bluey's spittle obviously contained every bacterium known to science, my frantic mother concluded that the local doctor would not be enough. I think I went to some kind of hospital . . . [where] needles were stuck into me while she had yet another case of heart failure. Bluey was taken away to be destroyed. Looking back on it, I can see that this was tough on Bluey, who had grown old in the belief that biting ankles was the thing to do. At the time I was traumatized. I loathed dogs from that day forward. They could sense my terror from miles away. Any dog could back me against a wall for hours. Eventually I learned not to show fear. The breakthrough came when I managed to walk away from a dog who had me bailed up against the door of a garage. Admittedly he was only a Pekingese about eight inches long, but it was still a triumph. That was more than a year ago.

■ CLIVE JAMES,
UNRELIABLE MEMOIRS

First he was a fierce, canine little beast, a beast of rapine and blood. He longed to hunt, savagely. He lusted to set his teeth in his prey. It was no joke with him. The old canine Adam stood first in him, the dog with fangs and glaring eyes. He flew at us when we annoyed him. He flew at all intruders, particularly the postman. He was almost a peril to the neighborhood. But not quite. Because close second in his nature stood that fatal need to love, the *besoin d'aimer* which at last makes an end of liberty. He had a terrible necessity to love, and this trammeled the native, savage hunting beast which he was. He was torn between two great impulses: the native impulse to hunt and kill, and the strange, secondary, supervening impulse to love and obey.

■ D.H. LAWRENCE,
"REX"

113

Lord Salisbury . . . asked me for the weekend to his country seat, Hatfield House. On a Friday afternoon I drew up before the ancient pile, built by Salisbury's ancestor, Sir Robert Cecil, first minister to Queen Elizabeth and James I.

I paid off the taxi and timidly rang a doorbell. To my surprise, Lady Salisbury, a gray-haired lady with a strong ancestral face, answered the bell. With her was an enormous hound, which looked at me in a markedly unfriendly fashion and growled. . . .

Lady Salisbury . . . saw that I was nervous. "Don't worry," she said. "Bobo never bites a gentleman, only tradesmen and the lower classes."

At this point, Bobo lunged forward and planted his teeth in my right calf.

■ STEWART ALSOP

Natural bitees are people whose approaches to dogs (and perhaps to people as well) are contaminated by epistemology. They attempt to *infer* whether or not the dog will bite, jump up on them or whatever. Instead of "reading" the dog, as handlers say (the German philosopher Martin Heidegger might call this listening to the dog's being), they cast about for some premise from which they can draw an inference that will give them certainty about the dog's behavior. They are—sometimes only momentarily—incapable of beholding a dog. It is not that the required information will follow too slowly on their observations, but that they *never* come to have any knowledge of the dog, though they may come to have knowledge *that*—knowledge that the dog is an Italian Spumone or a Komondor, for example. And dogs read this with the same uneasiness we feel when we walk into a room and find that our spouse, or a friend, has plainly been sitting around inferring something about us—welcome has been withheld. This creates in dogs and people an answering skepticism, an answering terror. The dog starts casting about for premises, making inferences back, tries to reach certainty, fails to reach certainty and sometimes bites, just as we do. Most dogs, however, express this uneasiness by trying to reassure us with affection, and dogs are astoundingly good at demolishing skeptical terror, which is why they are so often effective in therapy even when the therapist doesn't suspect that epistemology is the disease. Dogs in general are more skilled at belief than we are.

■ VICKI HEARNE,
ADAM'S TASK

I am driven mad by dogs, who have taken it into their accursed heads to assemble every morning in the piece of ground opposite, and who have barked this morning for five hours without intermission; positively rendering it impossible for me to work.

■ CHARLES DICKENS,
LETTERS

114

MONDO
CANINE

A dog who misbehaves after being left at home is acting not from spite but from separation anxiety. Dogs are pack animals and instinctively feel uncomfortable about being alone. Studies have shown that misbehavior most often occurs the first half-hour they are alone, when the stress of separation is the strongest.

■ WAYNE KIRN,
1990 365 DOGS CALENDAR

Bitches have a peculiar way when they are present at a meeting of two dogs equal in strength and rank. On such occasions Wolf's wife Susi certainly hopes for a fight; not that she helps her husband actively, but she likes to see him thrash an opponent. I have twice watched her adopt a most deceitful ruse in order to achieve this end. Wolf was standing head to tail with another dog—each time it was an outsider, a "summer visitor"—and Susi prowled round them carefully and interestedly, the dogs in the meantime taking no notice of her as a bitch. Then, silently but vigorously, she nipped her husband in his hindquarters, which were presented to the foe. Wolf assumed that the latter, by an intolerable breach of the age-old laws of canine custom, had bitten his posterior while sniffing it, and fell on him immediately. Since the attack appeared to the other dog an equally unforgivable contravention, the ensuing battle was unusually grim.

115

■ KONRAD LORENZ,
MAN MEETS DOG

Caliban had one abiding hatred: cats. Whereas the other dogs chased them joyously, or ignored them as inferior creatures, Caliban loathed them, chased them savagely, killed them mercilessly. He had a short, brutal way of doing it; if he caught a luckless cat—and he would run like a yearling buck, that dog Caliban—he would give it one shake, like the crack of a whip, and then toss the cat into the air. It usually died with a broken neck and a broken back. And by the law of the survival of the fittest, the cats that escaped from Caliban's savage sallies were wise in their generation and kept out of his way.

■ EMMA-LINDSAY SQUIER,
"THE SOUL OF CALIBAN"

Bonzo . . . was savage with stangers but docile toward friends of the family, and he not only knew me well but would greet me politely and even enthusiastically whenever our paths happened to cross. I was once invited to tea at Schloss Altenberg, the home of Bonzo and his mistress. I drew up on my motorcycle in front of the castle, which occupies a lonely position in the forest. I had dismounted and, with my back to the door, was bending down to adjust the stand of the machine, when Bonzo shot out and, quite understandably failing to recognize my over-all-clad backside, seized my leg in his teeth and hung on in true bulldog style. I yelled out his name in agonized tones, whereupon he fell as though shot by a gun and groveled before me on the ground. As there had obviously been a misunderstanding and as in any case my thick outfit had prevented serious injury—a few bruises on the shinbone do not matter to a motorcyclist—I spoke encouragingly to Bonzo, caressed him and was ready to forget it. But not so the bulldog. The whole afternoon he followed me round and at tea he leaned against my leg. Every time I looked at him he sat up very straight, fixed on me his protruding bulldog eyes and pleaded forgiveness by frantically offering his paw. Some days later when we met in the road, he did not greet me in his usual boisterous fashion, but in the same attitude of humility, giving me his paw, which I shook heartily.

■ KONRAD LORENZ,
MAN MEETS DOG

The family of my ninth-grade girlfriend had a Weimaraner once for about a week. When it tried to eat down their house, they had to let it go live in a place where it could be outside on a lot of land. Kathy's mother was extremely neat and they had a beautiful home at the end of a long paved lane, set back among some mature hardwoods. Anyway, their Weimaraner was even more intense than normal. One night Kathy's mother put him in the laundry room to sleep. Maybe he wouldn't make a mess in there. She put everything up that he might get to. She put a clean little rag rug down for him to lie on.

That rambunctious dog got hungry sometime in the middle of the night, and when he couldn't find anything to eat in the laundry room, he ate right through the wall into the kitchen. When Kathy's dad came down for his morning coffee he saw above the kitchen table what looked like a mounted Weimaraner head on the wall, except that it was moving.

■ PETER JENKINS,
CLOSE FRIENDS

If you want to cure your dog's bad breath, just pour a little Lavoris in the toilet. ■ JAY LENO

117

He thrusts me himself into the company of three or four gentlemen-like dogs, under the duke's table: he had not been there—bless the mark!— a pissing while, but all the chamber smelt him. "Out with the dog!" says one: "What cur is that?" says another: "Whip him out" says the third: "Hang him up" says the duke. I, having been acquainted with the smell before, knew it was Crab, and goes me to the fellow that whips the dogs: "Friend," quoth I, "you mean to whip the dog?" "Ay, marry, do I," quoth he. "You do him the more wrong," quoth I; " 'twas I did the thing you wot of." He makes me no more ado, but whips me out of the chamber. How many masters would do this for his servant? Nay, I'll be sworn, I have sat in the stocks for puddings he hath stolen, otherwise he had been executed; I have stood on the pillory for geese he hath killed, otherwise, he had suffered for't. Thou thinkest not of

MONDO
CANINE

SORRY...

The Romans called it *excrementum canis,* and it's been a problem since dogs and people began living together. It's especially troublesome on crowded city sidewalks—New Yorkers' famous head-down walking style may have its origin in trying to avoid it, and Londoners treat it with typical reserve:

STREET INSPECTOR PARR: Good afternoon, madam. I'm from the London Borough of Camden.

WOMAN: Yes?

INSPECTOR PARR: I was just standing at the corner of the road, observing. I saw your dog . . .

WOMAN: Yes?

INSPECTOR PARR: . . . foul the footpath.

WOMAN: Did you?

INSPECTOR PARR: Yes. Allow me to show my authority.

WOMAN: Oh, I'm sorry. I'm afraid we just, we had just bumped into one another on the street corner.

PARR: Yes. Well, I will point out where the dog has deposited. It is your dog?

WOMAN: Yes, it is. Yes.

PARR: You are aware that it is an offense to allow the dog to foul the footpath?

WOMAN: It's something very difficult, actually, to prevent a dog from doing.

PARR: Yes, I appreciate . . .

WOMAN: I . . . I . . . Oh, I also appreciate it's not very nice, you know, to have it deposited on the footpath, but it's very, very difficult to stop an animal.

PARR: It is your dog?

WOMAN: Yes, it is my dog. Yes.

PARR: I notice that you have it on a lead. I will point out the offense to you, madam. It's an offense against the bylaws of the London Borough of Camden.

WOMAN: Yes. Well, I accept that—but you know, it is very, very difficult. And he is normally trained to use the gutter.

PARR: Your remarks have been noted and I will incorporate them in my report. I now have to tell you the facts will be reported to the town clerk for his consideration.

■ *"60 MINUTES"*

this now. Nay, I remember the trick you served me when I took my leave of Madam Silvia: did I not bid thee still mark me and do as I do? When didst thou see me heave up my leg and make water against a gentlewoman's farthingale? Didst thou ever see me do such a trick?

■ WILLIAM SHAKESPEARE,
THE TWO GENTLEMEN OF VERONA,
ACT IV, SCENE 4

Milton Kagen was tired of dogs relieving themselves in his front yard in the Hollywood Hills while the mutts' masters watched placidly. So he posted a sign warning that his plants are sprayed with "dioxinleuco-maine." And since then, he adds, dog owners seem to "be getting the message."

Hold on a minute. Dioxinleucomaine? What's that? (Our computer spell checker nearly burst into flames.) "I made up the word," Kagen proudly admitted. ■ STEVE HARVEY

MONDo
CANINE

THE TROUBLE
WITH PIT BULLS

Pit bulls are responsible for the majority of dog-attack deaths in the United States, yet they constitute only a small portion of the total canine population. Most of these attacks are savage, unprovoked, and usually on children or elderly women. Municipalities have begun enacting legislation against pit bulls, and a few pit bull owners have been sent to jail for assault and manslaughter.

The American pit bull terrier, a medium-sized, short-haired breed, was first used to herd livestock, later in bull-baiting, and eventually for fighting. As a result, these dogs have combativeness in their genes. They are not inherently mean, but they are sturdy, tenacious, easy to train, and eager to please their human handlers. They are bred for "gameness," the ability to lock their jaws onto an adversary and not let go even if they go into shock due to injuries. They fight hard, and they fight to the death. Like other breeds, they can be trained to attack humans if that's what their owners want. Unlike other breeds, whose average jaw pressure is a few hundred pounds, pit bulls can exert jaw pressure of two thousand pounds.

The trouble with pit bulls is that some breeders mate mean dogs to mean bitches in order to produce entire litters of vicious hybrids. They are creating strains of uncontrollable canine psychopaths. The fault is in the breeders and in the people who buy these dogs for self-protection without knowing how to control them. The fault is not in our dogs, but in ourselves.

Rock hound: Coco's vet, Dr. David Stroshine of Salinas, California, holds 13 rocks swallowed by the one-year-old Labrador retriever. The dog was brought in for an upset stomach and required surgery to remove the rocks. Coco subsequently consumed more rocks and required another operation, prompting Dr. Stroshine to advise the dog's owners to keep her in a rock-free environment.

THE VET

STEVE SMITH

 Among the experiences a man shares with his hunting dog, the thoughts of days afield, exquisite points, or flawless retrieves through gale winds and smashing surf are probably the first—and most pleasant—to come to mind.

Yet, there are other experiences, ones we allow to fleet only briefly across our collective psyche. These experiences are less than memorable, and, in truth, are often harrowing for both man and canine. Topping my personal list of these dubious days of dogdom is a visit to the Vet.

Now, a dog that can't, after three years of yard training, learn the meanings of the words "come," "whoa," and "heel" will learn, after one trip to the pooch health parlor, not only what the word "vet" means, but he will learn to spell it as in: "Catch the dog because I'm taking him to the v-e-t." After this statement, Sport vanishes like snowflakes in a campfire.

A dog you thought couldn't smell a grouse if the bird moved in with him can smell the alcohol/disinfectant odor of the vet's office from 300 yards upwind.

And, a dog that has impeccable field manners is reduced to the four-footed equivalent of a juvenile delinquent within microseconds of entering the waiting room. In short, the average dog desires a trip to the vet as much as his owner covets hemorrhoid surgery.

So that I will not be accused of making all this up, I have decided to set down in print the latest bout I had with my faithful, nonslip, English pointer, Toby, during a recent trip to the Vet. I have recorded all times and events as they happened with no embellishments. See if this doesn't sound like your typical trip. Since I was busy most of the time, my notes are cryptic at best.

8:45 A.M.—Announce to wife that it is time for booster shot to be inflicted on Dog. Wife laughs in high-pitched, somewhat hysterical manner, her left eye starting to twitch.

8:47 A.M.—I locate Dog under bed in the spare bedroom, paws wrapped around bed frame and glazed look in eyes. I must take bed apart to separate Dog from furniture.

9:12 A.M.—Dog and I arrive at Vet's office. Dog holds onto steering wheel of Jeep as I attempt to remove him from vehicle. I am amazed at strength of this animal, strength of steering column of AMC vehicles, but disappointed in strength of new leather leash which breaks in scuffle.

9:15 A.M.—Enter Vet's office. I am dragging Dog behind me with remnants of leash. Dog pushes ahead of him three metric tons of gravel from Vet's parking lot due to the fact that he has not taken a step since leaving Jeep. I tell little teenage receptionist that I am here and wait while she pulls Dog's file and places it on desk. I notice that Dog's file is the only one of all those assembled with large black spot in upper right hand corner. I comment on this, and receptionist smiles wanly and excuses self to answer a phone which I could swear wasn't ringing.

9:20 A.M.—Seated in waiting room, I try to read magazine (circa 1948). Dog attempts to pick a fight with male half of a matched pair of grey French poodles. I separate animals after Dog has shredded hand-knitted sweater that Pierre (for this is the name of the beast) is wearing. I note with some relief that Dog has not perpetrated any ungentlemanly acts on Fifi, the female half of the poodle tandem.

9:21 A.M.—Dog attempts ungentlemanly act with Fifi. I intervene, prevent this mishap, and get glass of water for female owner of poodles who apparently suffers from an asthmatic condition.

9:26 A.M.—Dog has suddenly become a model of decorum, resting between my feet on the floor. Decorum has something to do with the recent entrance (at 9:25) of a Great Dane with the physical dimensions of large, chest-type freezer. Dane lies at his owner's feet and glares at Dog, who has taken a sudden interest in his toenails.

9:35 A.M.—I enter Vet's examination room. I wait quietly as Dog eats draperies suspended from window frame. Vet enters and asks me to place Dog on slippery, stainless steel examination table. Dog likes this about like I enjoy pulling my own teeth. Finally, I catch Dog (thanks to small size of room) and place him on table. Vet approaches.

9:38 A.M.—Vet notes that Dog is disgustingly healthy and will no doubt live many years. I am unsure of how I should take this news, as Vet tells me this with no discernible enjoyment. Vet approaches with Parvovirus serum in syringe. Dog looks as though the Second Coming has arrived and all the good hiding spots are occupied. I grapple with Dog. Vet grapples with Dog. Vet drops syringe. Vet glares at me and Dog. Dog glares back. I turn away and examine what is left of drapes.

9:41 A.M.—Vet has fresh syringe and look of determination—nay, vindication—on his face. Vet injects Dog with technique and enthusiasm akin to that of Olympic javelin thrower. Dog vocally carries on as though an important appendage is being amputated. I comment on this, and Vet notes that this wouldn't be a bad idea, although sound of Dog has covered his words so I cannot swear that he uttered that exact phrase.

9:44 A.M.—Dog and I emerge from examination room and visit teenaged receptionist who—until this very morning—had once entertained dreams of becoming a Vet. I pay bill and leave. As door closes behind me, I hear faint but growing crescendo of applause.

9:54 A.M.—I arrive home and Wife notes that Vet called and I have left remains of leash in waiting room. Vet also told Wife that I needn't return for the leash. He will mail it to me—at his expense.

Sam, the lead dog in the 1989–90 Trans-Antarctica Expedition. According-ing to team leader Will Steger, "Sam is the spark plug on the team . . . he gets the other dogs going because his spirit is so contagious."

DOGS AT WORK

Here were many men, and countless dogs, and Buck found them all at work. It seemed the ordained order of things that dogs should work. All day they swung up and down the main street in long teams, and in the night their jingling bells still went by. They hauled cabin logs and firewood, freighted up to the mines, and did all manner of work that horses did.
■ JACK LONDON,
THE CALL OF THE WILD

Dogs have been earning their keep since they began guarding Stone Age cave dwellings. Plutarch recounts the story of a watchdog at the Temple of Aphrodite who captured a thief after chasing him for twenty miles, and guard dogs were used in ancient Pompeii, as evidenced by the *"cave canem"* ("Beware of the Dog") signs that still appear on the houses.

Dogs are used as beasts of burden, for tracking, and in search-and-rescue operations. There are sled dogs and dogs who sniff out bombs, drugs, and even termites. And herding dogs have been used for centuries and are still at work on farms and ranches all over the world.

It's hard to believe how tough [herding] dogs are. And on this property they work in extreme conditions in all types of weather. Even with a dog in those sort of conditions, everything might be against him. He might have cut feet; he might have snowballs built up on him. They will always try and run; they will always try their best to do and complete the job you've put in front of them.
■ GRANT CALDER ON
"THOSE WONDERFUL DOGS"

The Border collie's natural herding instinct allows it to handle up to several hundred sheep alone, primarily by means of a mesmerizing stare known as the "eye."

■

American sheep ranchers use guard dogs to protect sheep from predators. Pups are "raised" by sheep and thereby develop a stronger bond with sheep than with humans or other dogs.

■

Rottweilers were used as drovers in Germany. They would herd the cattle to market and then guard the sale proceeds in pouches around their necks.

■

Dalmations began as companions to ancient charioteers, then served as coach dogs in Elizabethan England before assuming their present role as firehouse mascots.

Courtesy of Australian Overseas Information Service/John McKinnon

The Australian kelpie sheep dog was bred to meet the need for a dog with the stamina to run all day, short hair to stay cool in high temperatures, the discipline to bark at sheep without biting them, and the intelligence to think for itself. They are usually tan, or tan and black, and stand around 18 to 20 inches tall—except when on the backs of yarded sheep.

Dogs can be used as pack animals on thin snow crust that heavier animals such as donkeys or horses would break through.

■

There's a statue in Central Park to Balto, a Malamute who led a dog team through a blizzard to deliver diphtheria antitoxin to Nome, Alaska.

■

Amundsen's Arctic expedition took more dogs than needed to pull the sleds: the men and the surviving sled dogs consumed the weaker canines as they faltered.

SCENT WORK

A man can sit in his living room and tell you he smells nothing at all; at least he is conscious of no odors. Give him a whiff of frying ham, and he thinks he smells that and nothing else. So if his nose is selective, it is crudely so, and he records nothing but the exceptional odors. But visually he is highly selective, and he'll find a small object of interest in a vast scene containing a thousand larger things. The dog's nose is as selective as the man's eyes.

■ CHARLEY WATERMAN,
GUN DOGS & BIRD GUNS

Dogs experience the world through their noses. They have many times the number of olfactory cells that humans have, and so their sense of smell is hundreds or, in some breeds, thousands of times better than ours. While their noses do not respond to certain smells—flowers, for instance—they are extremely sensitive to the chemicals contained in human sweat, hence they are good at tracking and finding people. Search-and-rescue dogs have been used to find victims of avalanches, floods, and earthquakes, and to locate lost hikers and campers. Dogs are used to detect natural gas leaks and to scent truffles (unlike pigs, they do not *eat* the truffles when given the chance, though only mongrels or terriers are used because purebreds are distracted by any small game in the vicinity). And dogs are routinely used by law enforcement agencies to track fugitives and to detect bombs, firearms, and illegal drugs.

■

The U.S. Agriculture Department employs a brigade of beagles at airports throughout the country to sniff out contraband fruit hidden in passenger luggage.

■

Dogs have been used to determine whether twins are identical or fraternal because identicals have the same scent, but fraternals do not, no matter how much they may look alike.

130

On the trail the scent hound is seeking particulate matter, bits of dead skin that have scraped off the fleeing or wandering youngster. It scrapes away with every movement and floats to the ground. The armpits and crotch are particularly rich mines for this material, which is in fact the scent trail. The areas where the limbs meet the torso create unique smells, apparently, in every human being. So the running person, even the walking person, acts like a bellows spraying the ground with microscopic bits of self. Along comes the dog and those bits forge into a chain and become a trail. And trails are for running.

■ ROGER CARAS,
A CELEBRATION OF DOGS

An extraordinary number of failures at formal tracking trials happen when the handler pulls the dog away from the trail, which may be one of the reasons the bigger, stronger dogs do so well at tracking.

■ VICKI HEARNE,
ADAM'S TASK

Even the most skillful professional handler will occasionally yield to the temptation of asserting his intellectual superiority over the dog. More often than not, it is the handler who defeats the dog, rather than the difficulty of the trial.

■ L. WILSON DAVIS,
GO FIND!

Madge, a bitch owned many years ago by Dr. C. Fosgate of Oxford, New York . . . was once called upon to trace a lost boy in a town upstate. The trail was twenty-four hours old. Madge climbed fences, wandered through yards, went down alleys, and presently asked to be let into a grocery. Inside, she trotted to a crate of oranges, then crossed over and placed both front paws on the counter. The grocer then remembered that a little boy had come in the morning before, taken an orange from the crate, and paid for it at the counter. The end of the trail was tragic: Madge came to a pier end at a river and plunged unhesitatingly into the water. The boy had been drowned there.

■ JAMES THURBER,
"LO, HEAR THE GENTLE BLOODHOUND!"

131

The scent lay heavier there. He shuffled round over it, sifting the dust with an audible clapping of his nostrils to work out the pattern the man had made. It wasn't like any dust he had ever come across, either, being glittery, like mica, and slivery in his nose. But he could tell after a minute how the man had lain, on his back, with his hands under his head, and probably his hat over his eyes to shield them from the glare, which was pretty dazzling bright up this high, with no trees handy.

■ WALTER D. EDMONDS,
MOSES

You can have ten people enter a room and mill about in it for a while, then one of them leaves. When you bring your tracking dog into the room and ask her to search, she may very well nose about for a while, sorting things out, and then take off after the missing person. There

have been tests involving skunk spray, solutions of alcohol, formalde-
hyde and such, in which sebum and hair clippings were preserved for
several years. Trained dogs did not fail to match an object on which a
few drops of the solution were released with an article handled by the
person whose hair had been used in the first place.

■ VICKI HEARNE,
ADAM'S TASK

POLICE DOGS

Dogs were first used for police work in Germany in about 1900, and in the U.S. since
the end of World War II.

Rondo, a German shepherd police dog in Greenwood Village, Colorado, rescued
several children in a convenience store who were held at gunpoint by a drug-crazed
woman. "It was becoming a decision to shoot her or not," said Sgt. Walt Clark. "We
sent Rondo in. He was shot in the foot. He pursued her and took her to the ground.
In reality, he saved her life."

■

Two drug-sniffing U.S. Border Patrol dogs, Rocky and Barco, have been credited
with 187 cases involving heroin, cocaine and marijuana with a total street value of
$130 million. They've been so effective that smugglers have reportedly put a $30,000
bounty on their heads.

■

The Connecticut State Police use dogs trained to pick up the scent of decomposed
bones.

■

A bloodhound named Nick Carter was probably the all-time world's champion
tracking dog. He was directly responsible for over 700 arrests during his career as a
tracker for the Lexington, Kentucky, Police Department.

Rinnie and his handler, John Judge . . . were the pride of the Wichita, Kansas, Police Department. Rinnie's nose was foolproof; his heart gallant, brave and dedicated; his mind alert and questioning.

One night Chuck Smith, who had the job of collecting supermarket receipts and placing them in the night deposit at the bank, called the police to report that he had been kidnapped in his own car and robbed. The police asked Smith to take his car back to the point where the kidnapper had gotten out of it, and Rinnie and John Judge were dispatched to track down the villain. Rinnie, on arrival, was asked to search the car. After taking a good sniff, the dog, calmly and without hesitation, walked around the car to where the victim was talking with police officers, and bit him in the seat.

The comedy was lost on John Judge, who was flabbergasted and chagrined. He took Rinnie severely to task, and the dog was disgraced. While Smith was taken to the hospital, John Judge and Rinnie went back to headquarters. The news about Rinnie's mistake spread like wildfire and was featured by all of the news media: "Rinnie's misdeed was a welcome event for the anti-dog faction. Letters were dispatched to the chief and the mayor. A thorough investigation of the incident was requested, and Rinnie was suspended from the force. The Canine Corps was in jeopardy."

It is important to notice that the mistake was conceived of as an extraordinarily clumsy one, unworthy of "the most inexperienced police dog." This matters because it indicates the depth of the loss of faith, the darkness of soul, of the moment when John Judge reprimanded Rinnie. When a police dog bites a victim, the perdition of the handler is absolute. The center does not hold, things fall apart. The dog's potential for virtue, and for lapse, is greater than the policeman's for lapsing from human law.

Fortunately the story goes on. A minor character (one of the detectives who is not named in the account I read) delved into Smith's background

133

and had Smith submit to a lie-detection test. The machine, like the dog, said that he was lying, and further investigation revealed that Smith and an accomplice had planned the robbery together. (The significance of the parallel between the machine and the dog, and the fact that the machine's authority was higher than either John Judge's or Rinnie's, belongs to another discussion.) At the end of the story, John Judge and Rinnie are restored to honor, the criminals are in prison, and order is restored, that is, by the reaffirmation and acknowledgment, on the part of humanity, of the moral meaningfulness of the dog's actions.

■ VICKI HEARNE,
ADAM'S TASK

(c) Mark Wolgin

Officer Rick Miglia and his partner, Dandy, a K-9 cop responsible for one of the largest seizures of cocaine on record. Dandy's superb credentials as a drug-sniffer persuaded a judge to issue a search warrant for the suspect premises in Sylmar, California. The search uncovered over 20 tons of cocaine and $12 million in cash.

There was a twelve-year-old girl in Arcadia who took a handful of sleeping pills. The local police arrived on the scene and found the empty bottle and a suicide note, but the girl had disappeared. The doctor said that if she wasn't found within minutes the girl would be dead. The police department put 10 or 15 officers on it—it was a big mansion on a hillside—they walked all over the grounds several times and still couldn't find her. My fellow officer arrived with Arko, they gave him the circumstances, and he began to search the house. They said, "No, no, we already searched the house several times—you're wasting your time." Well, Arko went right to a closet and dragged the girl out from under a pile of clothing by her shoe and saved her life.

■ OFFICER RICK MIGLIA,
MONROVIA, CALIFORNIA,
POLICE DEPARTMENT

S E R V I C E   D O G S

There are many programs throughout the United States in which dogs are brought into hospitals, nursing and old age homes, and mental institutions. Puppies are often used because they are even more accepting and uncritical than adult dogs—they don't seem to care if a patient has a debilitating condition. They bring the patients out of themselves, giving them respite from their pain and isolation. "Social dogs" are used with autistic children, and it seems that stutterers don't stutter when they talk to a dog. Dogs are increasingly employed as Seeing Eyes, Hearing Ears, and Canine Companions.

The dog is therapeutic. Companion animals lower blood pressure in most people. Those people who have managed to create that bond that can exist between a human being and an animal tend to live longer, have fewer heart attacks, get fewer diseases, and, when they do get

Service dogs are trained to help a variety of disabled people, including the hearing-impaired and those confined to wheelchairs. Here, Oregon, a service dog trained by Canine Companions, Inc., takes the phone off the hook for her wheelchair-bound mistress.

sick, suffer less and get well quicker than others. Children growing up with pets they love and care for seem to turn out to be good parents and perhaps more selfless mates.

■ ROGER CARAS,
A CELEBRATION OF DOGS

An NIH facility that raises chimps for research used canine nannies to provide companionship for young chimps who have been rejected by their mothers.

■

Harley, a golden retriever owned by Victoria Doroshenko, warns his epileptic owner whenever she is about to have a seizure, long before the onset of visible symptoms. It is not known how Harley is able to do it; he may detect small behavioral changes not apparent to humans, or he may even have an innate sensitivity to changes in brain waves. In any case, Ms. Doroshenko is grateful: "Before I got my dog I was afraid and housebound. Harley gave me my life back."

■

The first Seeing Eye dog was a German shepherd bitch named Buddy, bred in Switzerland by Dorothy Eustis for police and rescue work. In 1928 Eustis invited a blind man from Tennessee named Morris Frank to Switzerland to work with one of her dogs. Frank and Buddy learned to work together during a five-week training period. On one occasion she dragged him away from a pair of runaway horses. When, at the end of the training period, they went to the village alone so Frank could get a haircut, he was jubilant at the simple act of independence. Frank and Buddy returned to the United States and toured the country on behalf of Seeing Eye, Inc., which was founded in 1929. Buddy occasionally helped herself to hors d'oeuvres at receptions and acknowledged applause by barking at the audience. During her years with Frank, Buddy saved him from a hotel fire and an open elevator shaft, and she once towed him to shore when he tired during a swim.

The dogs shuffling through each stop read the streets and hedges and utility poles. These dogs know when something is new. The trash can,

MONDO CANINE

137

the parked car, break up the picture in their heads. River pilots and the river. Their noses scour out a new channel, revise the map they carry in their bones. They pull their owners along the cluttered streets. These dogs see through their memory.

■ MICHAEL MARTONE,
"SEEING EYE"

138

CANINE ATHLETES

Dogs are natural athletes. The sporting breeds—retrievers, pointers, terriers, spaniels—are, after all, *jocks*. They live to do what centuries of selective breeding has equipped them to do best: work out. But even mutts love to play, and there's a growing trend toward organized canine athletic competition.

■

Frisbee contests have become big business: there are regional and national championships sponsored by dog food companies, and local events all over the country are drawing enthusiastic participation.

■

"Fun Runs" team dogs with their masters in 5- and 10-K runs.

■

In Lure Coursing, "sighthounds" (Afghans, Irish wolfhounds, borzois, salukis, whippets) chase an artificial lure along a random course through an open field.

■

There are agility competitions, obedience and field trials, even weight-pulling contests like Buck's in *The Call of the Wild*; a St. Bernard named Brutus set the world record by pulling 5,220 pounds.

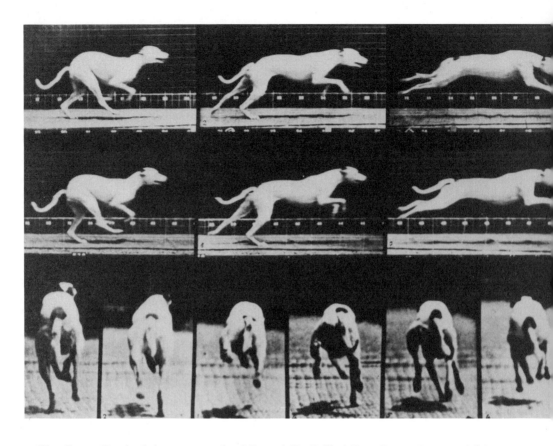

The Super Bowl of dog sports, the Iditarod Trail Sled Dog Race, is a punishing 1100-mile course from Anchorage to Nome. Four-time champion Susan Butcher calls her dogs "professional athletes."

I am thinking now of Hans, a Doberman, one of the most talented and competent dogs I have ever known. His response to the command "Fetch!" was so instantaneous, accurate and powerful that it sometimes seemed the air must ignite as he leaped forward from his handler's side. Among his more spectacular performances was the Drop-on-Recall. In

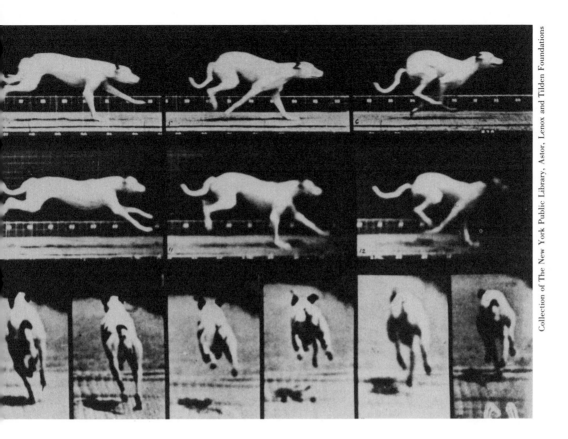

this exercise, as performed in competition, the handler tells the dog to stay and moves some thirty to fifty feet away, then turns and, facing the dog, commands, "Joe, Come!" When the dog has traveled some distance, usually about halfway, a drop command or signal is given, and the dog must drop to the ground and wait for a new recall command. With Hans it was generally necessary to say, "Hans, come down!" in one breath, for by the time the handler had finished pronouncing "come," Hans was already halfway home. And it was risky to perform the exercise on blacktop, since Hans responded to the command by

simply flattening out in midair and sliding, accepting like a base runner
the ripping of skin and joints the game of being a great dog entailed.

■ VICKI HEARNE,
ADAM'S TASK

H. Armstrong Roberts/DeBrocke (E.S.P.)

142

Racing greyhounds can reach speeds of 40 mph over a 500- to 1,000-
yard course. After a brief career they are no longer competitive and
become a liability: although they are very gentle, racing greyhounds
are not "socialized." They spend their entire lives in cages—many of
them don't even learn how to walk up a flight of steps. Thus they are
difficult to place as pets, and many of them are simply "destroyed"
upon their retirement from the sport.

Some notable canine athletes:

- Barkley, an Airedale who flies kites.
- Zack the Wonder Dog, a scuba-diving golden retriever.
- Zudnik, a wolf-Malamute who "skis" the Colorado Rockies with his master, Scott Kennett. Whenever Scott falls, Zudnik stops and waits impatiently to resume the run.
- A black Lab named Jessie who shoots pool.
- Cricket-playing dogs are a tradition in England. They actually play on human teams and a few have reached prominence: Old Wat was a sheepdog who, according to *Carr's Dictionary of Extra-Ordinary English Cricketers*, teamed with a Mr. Trumper of Harefield to defeat "two gentlemen of Middlesex in 1827." And, there was also Ponto, "the bravest of the Grace family dogs," who "fielded close in."

Los Angeles Times Photo by Ken Hively

Sidney, an English bulldog from Laguna Beach, California, was shown on national television hijacking a skateboard from a champion rider.

FROM *WE THINK THE WORLD OF YOU* BY J.R. ACKERLEY

It began simply enough. She was sitting on the divan facing me, staring at me, her long forelegs close together, the paw joints flexed over the edge of the bed. Sitting thus, she suddenly picked up her ball which, with various other objects to which she seemed to attach a value, she had collected about her, and set it on her legs. It rolled down them, as upon rails, fell to the floor and bounced across the room towards me. This was nothing. Pure accident. Merely amusing. The mechanics were easy; our relative positions directed the ball inevitably from her to me. Receiving it into my hand I returned it with a laugh. She caught it in her jaws. But then she set it on her legs again; down them it rolled, bounced across the carpet and reached my hand. Now I looked at her with more particularity and put my book away. The ball was in my hand, and she was gazing at me expectantly. For a second I hesitated, as though a cautionary hand had been laid upon me. Then I cast it back into her waiting jaws. She placed it upon her legs a third time. It did not move. Peering down at it, as if in perplexity, she gave it, with her long black nose, a shove, and it began once more its slow conversational journey from her to me. But now, just as it reached the verge—was it simply because she childishly felt she could not after all bear to part with it, or because the hitch that had occurred had vexed her?—she suddenly seized it back with a swift, almost scolding, thrust of her head and replaced it on her legs. It rolled. It fell. It bounced. It crossed the room and came into my hand. Yes, yes, of course, I know;

it is absurd to read too much into animal behaviour, and afterwards, as I have said, I laughed it off; but at that moment I did take the uncanny impression that, in a deliberate and purposeful way, she had gathered up all her poor resources and, in order to reach me directly and upon my own ground, had managed to cross that uncrossable barrier that separates man and beast. The expression on her face contributed to this fleeting illusion. Some animals have a furrow above their eyes very like that furrow, etched by a lifetime of meditation, that we see upon the brow of sages. In the animals' case, of course, it is merely the loose skin wrinkling upon the line of the socket bone; but it often imparts to their faces a similar look of wisdom. Evie had this 'intellectual' line, and it lent to her expression now an appearance of the profoundest concentration. With her nose pointing down and her ears cocked forward she followed, with the utmost gravity, the progress of the ball as it travelled down her legs, fell over the edge, bounded across the carpet and reached my hand; then, without altering the bent position of her head, she raised her eyes beneath their furrowed brows to mine and directed at me the kind of look that two scientists might exchange after successfully bringing off some critical experiment in physics. Yet, when I returned the ball to her now, it was as though the effort she had been making—if effort it was—suddenly failed; she became a mere dog once more, kicking up her legs and rolling about with the toy in her mouth; and when I offered, out of curiosity, to replay the game next evening, I could not get it going; she seemed worried and confused; the inspiration, having done its work, had apparently gone out of her forever.

King Arthur ("Artie" to his friends) is a 7-year-old yellow Lab who travels the country appearing at RV and sportsmen's shows billed as the "World's Most Intelligent Dog." According to his owner-trainer Lee LeCaptain, Artie can dive 20 feet underwater and hold his breath for three minutes, he can count and add anything up to ten, barking the answers out, and he can blink and sneeze on cue. But his greatest skill is his logrolling ability: "He's the Ashley Whippett of logrolling," boasts LeCaptain.

King Arthur (left) versus Lady Guinevere.

Rocky discovered his surfing ability at an early age, when his owner, Robin Marien, was pulling his surfboard along the beach: "All of a sudden I looked back and saw that Rocky was standing on it. I figured, Okay, what the hell, if that's what he wants. So I took him out, let him go, and he caught the wave the very first time."

Courtesy of Peter Bloeme and Irv Lander

FRISBEE DOGS

Why teach your dog to play Frisbee? There are many reasons:

1. It's a fantastic way to keep a dog in excellent condition by promoting cardiovascular development. The running and jumping involved in the sport improves muscular strength and prevents misdirected energy.

2. Frisbee is great for a dog's eyesight! While both improving and strengthening vision, it helps him track (follow) and focus on a small moving object.

3. It promotes camaraderie between owner and pet, and creates a special bond of friendship. It gives the dog a special reason for living.

4. Playing with a Frisbee and teaching your dog to play is a challenge for both of you. It offers an opportunity for you to share an interest as a team. And if you decide to compete, it can involve the whole family.

5. Frisbee competitions are open to all dogs regardless of breeding and size. Pound puppies can compete "paw to paw" with purebred canines.

Still, the most basic reason for teaching your dog to play is simply that dogs *love it!*

■ PETER BLOEME,
FRISBEE DOGS

Jeff Gabel and Casey

Bill Waters and Air Major

Ashley Whippett, the most famous canine sports star of all time. Acclaimed as the "Babe Ruth of frisbee dogs," Ashley had all the tools: speed, grace, superb eye-mouth coordination. His owner, Alex Stein, trained Ashley from a pup by feeding him all his meals in a frisbee.

HUNTING DOGS

Reason, which came to fill the gap left by the evanescent instincts, fails in the task of raising the suspicious game. For millennia man gave this difficulty a magical solution, and therefore, no solution at all. But one day he had an ingenious inspiration, and in order to discover the extremely cautious animal he resorted to the detective instinct of another animal; he asked for its help. This is the point at which the dog was introduced into hunting, the only effective progress imaginable in the chase, consisting, not in the direct exercise of reason, but rather in man's accepting reason's insufficiency and placing another animal between his reason and the game.

■ JOSE ORTEGA Y GASSET,
"MEDITATIONS ON HUNTING"

I like them all—pointers, setters, retrievers, spaniels—what have you. I've had good ones and bad of several kinds. Most of the bad ones were my fault and most of the good ones would have been good under any circumstances.   ■ GENE HILL

The history of every hunting dog that has become popular through the AKC show ring is the same—the dog has lost its working ability. The key to the problem is popularity. For example, the most popular dog in the country is the Cocker Spaniel. Once a great hunting dog, today the Cocker is useless in the field. It can't hunt its way to the meat counter in a supermarket. The Poodle was number two. It has been taken out of the duck marsh and made into a sissy. Its topknot is dressed in ribbons. The AKC English Setter's silky coat, down to its knees, would be ruined in a brier patch, and it has lost its nose. The Irish Setter has been made into a highstrung, blooming idiot. The list goes on. If the

MONDo
CANINE

men who started the AKC one hundred years ago could see what their organization has done to our hunting and also to our working dogs, they would turn over in their graves.

■ RICHARD A. WOLTERS,
DUCK DOGS

If you have done much chasing of bobwhite quail, you will recall days when you could not hit a flushing blanket with all four corners going in different directions. And when, after repeated misses, one of the old dogs turned from his lingering point and indignantly stared at you. Under such circumstances, I have seen a variety of eyes eloquently pleading for me to get on the stick or go home and sign up for skeet lessons.

■ CHARLEY DICKEY,
"HOW TO HELP A BIRD DOG"

I remember training one of my Labradors to do a rather difficult series of retrieves which involved going from land through water, over land and through water again to find a bird that she hadn't seen shot. Time and again she fell short of what I expected and both her patience and mine were beginning to fray a lot more than just around the edges.

Just about the time I began shouting like a maniac, out of pure frustration, the dog came back to within a few feet of me and waited until I had calmed down and then, through the expression on her face, told me as plainly as if she could speak, that she didn't really understand what I wanted her to do and that if I could find some way of explaining it, she'd be pleased to do it my way. And that's finally what happened.

■ GENE HILL,
"THE DOG MAN"

153

Joe's pointer, Lady, was one of those reliable, conscientious dogs who take work seriously. She was retrieving a quail for Joe when he hauled off with his old Fox and shot another one, which she encountered on the way back in. Now there are stories of dogs pointing birds with others in their mouths and there are stories of dogs bringing in two at once, but Lady had never studied those programs and she was confronted with what the military experts might term a problem in logistics. Here she was with one bird in her mouth and another bird that she wanted to take to Joe too.

After a brief survey of the situation with several changes of expression, Lady gulped hard, swallowing bird number one, and triumphantly turned toward Joe with bird number two in her mouth. But halfway in, while mentally reviewing the situation, Lady concluded she had done wrong. A look of canine consternation came to her face and she apologetically crawled the last twenty feet on her stomach.

■ CHARLEY WATERMAN,
GUN DOGS & BIRD GUNS

154

You tie a bird's wing or a rag on the end of the line, tie the line to an old fishing rod, and flop the wing in front of the pup. When he pounces, you whip the wing away. Don't let him catch it. He will start pointing the thing. He will probably do it when very young indeed. This is like watching one of those Japanese infants playing real Beethoven on the violin. You melt.

■ DATUS C. PROPER,
PHEASANTS OF THE MIND

Ninety-five percent of the . . . dogs in this country are flea bags and affectionate parasites. For nothing more than a little companionship, a wag of the tail, they get room and board, medical care, social security, plush living, unemployment compensation, plus your easy chair. What kind of a business deal is that? Your puppy is to be the worker— you the boss. Let's get that straight from the start. Eventually, if he

does his job well, he'll be made a full-fledged partner. If not, *get rid of him.*
                                   ■ RICHARD A. WOLTERS,
                                         GUN DOG

There were two dogs with us the night we went coon hunting. One was an old hound, veteran of a thousand campaigns, who knew what we were up to and who wasted no time in idle diversions. The other was a puppy, brought along to observe and learn; to him the star-sprinkled sky and the deep dark woods and the myriad scents and the lateness of the hour and the frosty ground were intoxicating. The excitement of our departure was too much for his bowels. Tied in the truck, he was purged all the way over to Winkumpaw Brook and was hollow as a rotten log before the night was well under way.
                                   ■ E. B. WHITE,
                                   "COON HUNT"

Jeff was a big golden retriever who lived to hunt pheasant. He would begin to shiver with anticipation the minute his master opened the closet door and reached for the shotgun. He would get even more frantic as preparations continued, and by the time the gear had been loaded into the car, he would be beside himself. Along the route to the game preserve his excitement would reach a fever pitch, and the car would have to be pulled over so he could get out and vomit—always at the same spot along the route (dogs being creatures of habit). Thus relieved, Jeff would become visibly calmer and more businesslike.

Jeff was an excellent bird dog and he performed his job with skill and enthusiasm. But when the hunt was over, he would become positively morose, almost belligerent. And he did not suffer novice hunters gladly: on one occasion I'm afraid I ruined Jeff's day. After having missed *all* my shots, I was handed his leash and was asked to lead him to the car, but Jeff stubbornly refused to budge. When I tugged harder he emitted a basso profundo growl that clearly said, "Pull me again, bozo, and I'll rip your throat out."

Eventually the gear was put back in the car and it was time to head for home. At his master's command, Jeff would get into the car slowly, as if he had aged considerably since that morning, when he had bounded into the back seat. He looked dejected, as if dreading the return to the safe, monotonous life of a family dog. Scrunched down in the back with his chin on his paws, he would fall into sullen sleep as the car turned onto the highway.　　■ HOWARD OGDEN

156

KELLY, HE

GOT THEM ALL

CHARLEY WATERMAN

 When we buried old Kelly, we put up a plaque with the names of 18 upland birds burned into it. He'd pointed all of them from Alaska to Mexico and I wrote a book about them.

To this day nobody else has come forth to announce that his dog has pointed all 18 major species of North American game birds so I guess it's more unusual than I thought at the time. There may be some who figure the list could be broken down further and some who think we overdid it but our figure comes to 18 kinds of birds, and I've heard no complaints.

Now, Kelly was a Brittany, a breed that comes on pretty slowly in the South where "bird dogs" are pointers with palmetto scratches on their ears. A Brittany is a spaniel that points like a setter. Kelly weighed about 38 pounds, was orange and white, fairly long-haired, and had a bobbed tail like other Brittanies. A male pointer will weigh 50 pounds or more in most cases and I have heard Kelly called a "little fuzzy dog." There is a lady who owns a quail plantation up near Monticello, is world famous for her fine pointers, and who calls Brittanies "snuffle pups." But she keeps a few of them around her place.

Frank Woolner, a famous gunner and author, is like some other bird hunters who feel a bird dog should have a long tail. Woolner wrote me that Brittanies work fine but he never could get used to shooting grouse over an Easter bunny. Kelly couldn't have cared less about such comments, figuring a pocket bird dog gets to make more trips, lives comfortably in a one-man mountain tent (with the man) and slides into a motel without attracting too much attention. Any canine who does all those things is likely to have personality and ideas of his own. Kelly did.

Take retrieving. Kelly would bring the bird if you couldn't get to it yourself but he reasoned that he didn't have hands and it was an imposition to expect him to carry things around when it was easier for you. Shoot a bobwhite in short grass and he wouldn't touch it but when I spilled a ptarmigan over an Alaska cliff he clattered down after it, down into the mists hell-bent, just hitting the rocks now and then. I never expected him to get back but he did, and he had the bird, clawing his way over the edge again. When he knew I could see it he threw it down and went hunting.

When he was a pup we took him with us to work on some planted, pen-raised quail along with some young pointers. That's when he pointed his first quail and was doing such a good job of it that the preserve operator, wearing polished boots, told me I should walk up, pat him and tell him he was a good dog. I did, although I was apprehensive. Kelly immediately lay down to have his belly scratched, to the amazement of a rigid pointer who was backing him. After getting the recognition he felt he deserved, Kelly wriggled happily, sniffed the grass and flowers with appreciation, then arose and again snapped into a classy point. The quail was surprised too, I think. I could see him plainly three feet away.

I don't shoot very well and Kelly was quite tolerant of me but he knew Buddy Nordmann was with it. After he gained experience he could make a federal case of pointing a single quail. He'd go through an elaborate stalking procedure, looking back at you as if to say, "Man, he's here and you'd better be ready!"

By the time Kelly actually pointed, many shooters would be a little unstrung. He did the whole bit for Buddy, who doesn't miss very much. On this one occasion Buddy missed—twice. Kelly watched the quail disappear into the old orange grove and then looked sorrowfully toward Buddy who was standing there in shock. Kelly's heart brimmed with compassion. He trotted back to Buddy, put his paws on Buddy's belt and looked sympathetically up into Buddy's red face.

Buddy reacted.

"Call off your damn dog!" he said.

Kelly charged hard when he hunted. That's how he broke his front leg, and that's why he'd get overheated on warm Florida days. He'd take frequent breaks, digging holes to cool off in, and places where he'd hunted frequently looked like old battlefields.

A quail went up high to clear some trees and I miraculously nailed it so that it plunged into an area where I couldn't mark it down. Kelly went in to look for it but he didn't come back and after a little whistling and yelling I went in to look for him. I finally found him flattened out on his stomach in a fresh hole. He looked up when I came floundering through the brush, and I made some remarks about his goofing off when there was a bird down. He reached over to where the bird was lying beside him and flipped the quail toward me with his nose.

Case closed.

He then cooled off for three or four minutes before going back to work.

159

He had a sense of humor. In his youth he continually ran afoul of skunks. He didn't hurt them, just managed to fool around until they doused him. There was once when my wife greeted me with a jug of vinegar as I dismounted from the truck.

"I smelled you when you turned in the driveway," she said. Kelly strolled over to get his bath.

Then Kelly decided skunks were a joke and he didn't get too close to them any more. There was the time when he pointed at the wreckage of an old wagon and I went over and kicked it. No doubt then as to what was hiding under the wagon and as I whirled about to escape I saw that Kelly was already 50 yards away where he had headed as I aimed the kick. He was grinning happily.

In some of the country we hunted there were quite a few porcupines. Some dogs repeatedly get quilled and I can dequill a dog blindfolded although it can be pretty tough on the dog. As far as I know Kelly never in all his life got a single quill in him.

Kelly always scorned Murphy, a big square-headed English pointer I used to hunt Hungarian partridge. Murphy wasn't much of a thinker and Kelly considered him a congenital idiot. He loved to see Murphy in trouble.

Murphy pointed at the edge of some brush and Kelly backed him gleefully and kept turning and looking at me as I hurried up from 200 yards away.

I couldn't hear him but I am sure Kelly said, "Boss, you gotta see this. Come on."

Then while I was still 50 yards away, Kelly tippy-toed up beside Murphy who was all charged up and quivering anyway.

"Yip!" said Kelly right in Murphy's ear, and Murphy charged.

Poor old Murphy landed right on a big, irritated porky and gave a pathetic howl of pain. Kelly disappeared and it was only when I got out the pliers and took a death grip on Murphy that he came back to watch me pull the quills. It made his whole day and he grinned ecstatically.

As he grew older, Kelly learned his combat limitations, but he had definite opinions of other dogs. He was peaceful most of the time, but there were certain dogs he didn't like and never would. One of these was Iron Mike, a larger Brittany who had spent his youth in the street and knew his way around. Mike was too big to fit the Brittany specifications, and I think a setter got under a fence somewhere in his ancestry, even though he was properly registered.

The feud really started when I somehow picked up Kelly after picking up Iron Mike from a friend's kennel. This was an insult. That was Kelly's truck. In somebody else's car he was the polite guest. To be greeted by a big ugly dog already in his own vehicle was too much, and on the way to the hunting grounds Kelly kept growling at a pitch seemingly far too low for so small a dog. He sounded a little like a stuck Jeep. Mike, who was not used to being pushed around, growled back.

They worked together all day but just before going in we put them down to hunt one more spot and apparently we put them out of the truck too close together. Maybe I set one of them on top of the other as I unloaded. Anyway, they turned into a blurred ball of brindle fur from which came sounds like feeding time at the zoo.

I am not too good at breaking up dog fights but I was hunting with Ben Williams who has spent some time as a professional dog trainer and we walked in with confidence.

I still have a scar on my leg to prove I tried. Ben got it through the hand and the whole thing turned into a bloody mess. We finally broke it up but neither dog was satisfied and to the day Kelly died we had to watch them closely.

As we patched up our wounds, Ben remarked that there had been times when Kelly was winning. Then he repeated the old saying.

"It's not the size of the dog in the fight. It's the size of the fight in the dog!"

A little mutt with fire can go awfully good for a while. Somebody let a yellow Lab get too close to Kelly's dish one time and Kelly had him pretty badly chewed up before we stopped it. Of course once the Lab got started, Kelly would have been only a tidbit. I'm really not bragging about having a fighting dog, but it was hard not to admire the little rascal.

"He'd have made a hell of a football player," a coach once told me.

But like other dogs who live with people and without other dogs around constantly, Kelly turned into something of a prima donna. He didn't eat very much and during hunting season we worried a little about it. Give him a doggie bone and he'd trot around and show it to everybody, then put it away somewhere.

Ben Williams, the aforementioned expert, visited our house one time when Kelly was ignoring his heaped dish.

"Trouble is," Ben said, "he has no competition for food and he enjoys being coddled and coaxed. Makes him feel important. Watch this."

So Ben got down on hands and knees and approached Kelly's dish. Kelly suddenly became attentive. His eyes popped. His tail stiffened.

Ben stopped at the dish and stuck his head down toward it.

"Slurp, glub, glub," said Ben.

Kelly looked at me in amazement and back at Ben. Ben got up and walked away. Kelly hurried to the dish and ate the whole thing rapidly with his eyes rolling apprehensively. This was a gratifying experience for me: it proved conclusively that we were just as smart as Kelly, maybe smarter.

Now if you are going to haul a dog all over the country to hunt all of those birds you need a good traveler. When Kelly was quite young, we got him a Miami Beach towel. It had palm trees and "Miami Beach" in big letters, and Kelly soon learned he was supposed to stay on that towel when living in motels. As time went on, he learned that as long as he could touch the towel everything was all right. He would take a pretty long lead like a guy edging off first base, but when anyone looked at him, he'd tag up again.

As the years went by, Kelly learned that he could leave his towel with impunity when he was alone. Oh, he'd never get on a bed or anything that would leave any incriminating evidence, but when you came back you'd hear him scramble to tag up again. The towel was getting pretty well worn when Kelly left us just before he was eight years old, but he never nibbled it or scratched it. That towel was important, even when he was a pup and a little hard on other softies he found lying around.

There are pointing specialists who learn only one or two birds. Kelly would point to anything after he learned we wanted it, but he always felt big birds were better. The toughest time I had keeping him in line was when I'd hunt valley quail (California quail) in chukar country.

The chukar is a cackling rascal who lives in the high, dry mountain country, sometimes adjacent to the bottoms and draws where quail stay. If Kelly was tending to business with the quail and happened to hear a chukar call, he'd slip off, going faster and faster, and head for the high places. Chukar were bigger and hence more important. After a little I'd see him parading around on a hillside trying to get me to follow him and the chukars.

And old Kelly would point woodcock. It took him only an hour or so to learn that business despite what folks say about the timberdoodle smelling different and having no attraction for dogs that haven't been trained for them.

The man I first went woodcock hunting with was a loyal pointer man and a good one, who asked if that little fuzzy dog would point birds. I didn't impress him with my answer and he figured my dog was going to be a nuisance. The pointers tended to put him down, too.

Well, Kelly found a woodcock, and a big handsome pointer backed him momentarily and then hunkered down and sneaked past Kelly like a Walt Disney animated snake. When the big pointer had passed Kelly, he stood up and stole the point. The pointer's owner walked in, kicked up the bird and downed it, called "Fetch!" and complimented me on my dog.

"That little fuzzy dog sure backs good," he said.

Thanks a lot.

A while later my new friend's big pointers failed to find a woodcock that was evidently trundling around in a grassy patch. After considerable careful shuffling they went off. Along came Kelly, operating on his own, checked the grass patch and nailed the woodcock. My friend kicked it up and shot it.

"That fuzzy little dog's tired," he said. "I'm going to put him back in the car."

He did, and Kelly spent the rest of the afternoon trying to dismantle the dog box and yelling bloody murder. Being banished was the final insult of a day of injustices.

It took me several years to shoot all of the upland birds of North America over Kelly. It started out by accident, and then I suddenly realized I had most of them and began to plan special trips.

Long ago Kelly went to where I like to think all of the bones are juicy and the birds never flush wild. They say a man is entitled to one good hunting dog in a lifetime. I guess I've had mine.

MONDO CANINE

DOG HEROES

The plain fact that my dog loves me more than I love him is undeniable and always fills one with a certain feeling of shame. The dog is ever ready to lay down his life for me. If a lion or tiger threatened me, Ali, Bully, Tito, Stasi and all the others would, without a moment's hesitation, have plunged into the hopeless fight to protect my life if only for a few seconds. And I?
■ KONRAD LORENZ,
MAN MEETS DOG

The trouble was that no self-respecting dog ever could see any reason why it should be afraid of a leopard. A leopard was hardly any bigger than itself and, in any case, was a species of cat which no dog could be expected to respect. When they had found themselves faced with a leopard, the dogs had had no hesitation in rushing to the attack. Unfortunately, leopards not only had teeth that were sharper than dogs and jaws that were just as powerful, but they were also armed with four sets of long, sharp claws as tough and piercing as steel. Dogs could not hope to match such heavy armament.
■ LAURENS VAN DER POST,
A STORY LIKE THE WIND

First, dogs will return love under almost any circumstances, unlike humans. Next, dogs are herd animals by instinct, so the humans around them become their pack, to be protected. And finally, some dogs are working dogs, and it's in their blood to save and even rescue.
■ YORAM HAMIZRACHI

Unless they are mistreated, and often in spite of abuse, dogs are steadfast, loyal friends, and in a sense all dogs are heroes: the typical family dog will guard his home

MONDO CANINE

against all intruders and fight to the death to protect family members from attack.

The record of canine heroism dates back to antiquity. The Romans staged fights between dogs and tigers in which the dogs often won. For three hundred years St. Bernards have been rescuing hikers and skiers. One named Barry saved forty-four people from a blizzard before the forty-fifth mistook him for a bear and shot him dead. There are countless examples of dogs saving people from fires, earthquakes, drowning, attacks by wild animals, land mines, kidnappers, even runaway trolley cars.

Why do they do it? What causes a dog to risk its life to save a member of another species? Should canine heroism be viewed anthropomorphically, or from a "behavioral" perspective? Do they save our lives because they care about us, or out of mindless instinct?

Some animal psychologists believe that dogs fail to perceive the risk of performing heroic deeds and that they wouldn't be so brave if they understood the danger. But those who know dogs and deal with them daily on a professional basis think that they do it out of selflessness, love, and loyalty.

Over the past fifty years in the United States there have been hundreds of newspaper accounts of canine heroism, including a bulldog killed while saving a boy being attacked by three Great Danes, a Labrador retriever who protected two small girls from an attack by a rabid raccoon, an Irish setter who braved flames to rescue a little girl from a burning car, an Airedale who ran seven miles home to get help for its wounded master, and a mutt who bit a man to keep him from entering a house filled with propane gas.

Since 1954 Ken-L Ration has presented an annual dog hero award. Of the forty-three persons saved by the Ken-L Ration dog heroes, fourteen were from near drownings, five from fires, five from animal attacks and three from traffic accidents. Some recent winners:

■

Tango, a thirteen-year-old mixed breed, had been saved from the pound when she was a pup by Al Choate of Port Townsend, Washington. An auto mechanic who raises livestock as a hobby, Al trained Tango to help him herd the few head of cattle he kept on his small farm. One morning Al and Tango were checking the livestock when the cow, acting to protect her newborn calf, charged at Al, knocked him to the ground, and began butting him. He sustained a punctured lung and several broken ribs but was saved from further injury when the fifty-pound Tango jumped in, bit into the cow's cheek and held on, allowing her master to crawl to safety. Asked about their dog's bravery, Mrs. Choate said, "Of course, we are overjoyed with the award. Tango is certainly deserving of it, but it wouldn't make any difference to us if she had won it or not. There isn't any price tag you can put on her. She's just a wonderful dog, the best friend we'll ever have."

■

Jet, a sixteen-year-old Doberman pinscher owned by Candy Sangster of Sepulveda, California, saved her owner's life when Candy passed out and slipped into a diabetic coma. Jet ran into the yard, unlatched the gate, ran next door, and began barking and running through the house, prompting the neighbor to call 911. Jet continued barking and darting between the houses until the paramedics arrived. "When I came to," Candy said, "I heard one of the paramedics say, 'This dog deserves a medal.' Now she has one. A friend gave us Jet when she was just eight weeks old. She's the best gift we've ever received."

■

Leo, a four-year-old, white standard poodle owned by William and Lana Callahan of Hunt, Texas, saved eleven-year-old Sean Callahan and his nine-year-old sister from a rattlesnake attack. The youngsters were playing along a creek bed when Sean stumbled over a six-foot diamondback. Leo jumped between the boy and the snake just as it struck, shielding the boy and taking several venomous bites. The Callahans rushed Leo to the vet, who administered antivenom. After hovering near death for several days, Leo eventually recovered.

■

King, a five-year-old German shepherd and husky mix, literally walked through fire to save his masters' lives. At 3:30 a.m. on December 22, 1980, Howard and Fran Carlson and their daughter Pearl were asleep in their home in Granite Falls, Washington, when flames from an electrical fire erupted in their kitchen and roared through the house. King entered the house from his outdoor sleeping area, ran into Pearl's bedroom, tore off the blankets, and began tugging at her arm, finally pulling her out of bed. Pearl ran screaming through the thick smoke into her parents' room. Fern woke her husband—who had recently been hospitalized with lung disease—led him to an open window, and told him to jump. Then she grabbed Pearl, who in the confusion had wandered into the living room. Fern opened another window, pushed Pearl out, and then jumped herself. At that moment King appeared at Pearl's window. He was trying to bark, but all he could manage was a squeak. Fern ordered King to jump, but when he ran back toward the master bedroom instead, Fran realized that Howard was still in the burning house. Fern made her way back through the smoke and flames toward the sound of King's whining and found Howard lying semiconscious on the floor. She helped him to his feet, and they managed to break open a sliding glass door and jump to safety, followed closely by King. "He was the last to leave," she said. "He wouldn't budge before we were outside."

It wasn't until daybreak that the Carlsons saw the singed hair on King's body and his burned, swollen paws. They discovered that his metal chain collar had become so hot it had burned his throat, preventing him from barking normally. And when King refused food, they found wood splinters in his mouth and realized that to save his family, King had gnawed through a plywood door.

■

Villa, a Newfoundland puppy purchased by Dick Veit and his wife Lynda of Villas, New Jersey, in February of 1982, adjusted to her new family quickly and even made friends with Andrea Anderson and her sisters Heather and Diane, who lived next door.

In 1983 a powerful blizzard struck southern New Jersey. On Friday, February 11, blinding snow and gale-force winds buffeted Villas, which is a beachfront community. School had been cancelled, so Andrea and her sisters bundled up and went outside. But Heather and Diane soon went back indoors, leaving Andrea to play in the snow by herself. The wind blew harder and colder, so Andrea decided that she too had had enough. As she started back to the house, a powerful gust threw her forty feet down an embankment into a deep snowdrift. With her vision obstructed by blowing snow and sand, buried up to her chest and unable to move, Andrea began crying and calling for help, but because of the howling wind, no one could hear. The more she struggled, the more desperate she became.

Meanwhile, Dick Veit had granted Villa's silent request to be allowed out; when Andrea began calling for help, the one-hundred-pound dog jumped a five-foot fence and made her way through the drifting snow to where the girl was trapped. Villa immediately began licking the frozen tears off the girl's face, then methodically tamped down the surrounding snow. Finally Villa stopped still and thrust her head toward the girl. Andrea got the message: she put her arms around Villa's neck and the dog pulled her out of the snowdrift. After an arduous trek in which it took fifteen minutes to cover forty feet, Villa returned the girl to her doorstep, then made her way back to her own house and collapsed exhausted by the fireplace.

■

Reona, a two-year-old Rottweiler, was named the 1989 Ken-L Ration dog hero of the year for saving the life of five-year-old Vivian Cooper during the 1989 San Francisco earthquake. When the tremors began, Reona heard the child's frantic screams from across the street. The dog bolted out of the house, jumped several fences, and dashed into the Coopers' kitchen, where Vivian was standing frozen with fear. Reona pushed Vivian out of the center of the room and then shielded the little girl with her own body. "Vivian is an epileptic, and the doctor had warned that any kind of upsetting experience could trigger a seizure," said Vivian's mother. "Somehow, Reona instantly grasped the situation. She turned to Vivian and gently nosed her up against the wall and held her there. It was an absolute miracle, because just then the heavy microwave oven came crashing down on the exact spot where Vivian had been not one second before. She certainly would have been killed. When the shaking stopped, I was finally able to get over to Vivian. I said to Reona, 'Can I have my baby back please?' Reona looked at me as if to say, 'Well, if you are calm enough.' Then she just walked out the door."

■

The list of dog heroes goes on and on. Such incidents are so common that many of them go unrecognized except for the love and gratitude of the dogs' owners. Some examples:

Chelsea, a golden retriever, was shot and wounded defending his master from armed robbers.

Ruffy, a collie-husky mix, saved his eighteen-year-old owner from an attack by a rabid fox. "My dog attacked the fox as it lunged toward me, knocking it down and fighting with it till I got away," said Kevin Hargreaves, who hit the fox with a stick, stunning it long enough to allow the police to get to the scene and shoot it.

Bella ran into his house and barked, cried, then tore out of the house, jumped over the backyard fence, dove into the neighbor's swimming pool, grabbed a drowning baby's hand, and paddled the infant to safety.

Bailey, a Labrador retriever, was practicing aquatic retrieving when his leg became tangled in some underwater brush. His owner swam out, extricated him from the brush, and began to swim to safety, but she soon became exhausted; Bailey, now free but with a severe gash on his hind leg, returned the favor by pulling her ashore.

Yogi, a five-year-old German shepherd, broke through a screen door to save his owner, Pat Morgan, from an attack by an intruder who had beaten her severely and was in the process of choking her. The dog held the man at bay until the police arrived. "If he had not managed to break into the house, I would have been choked to death," said Morgan.

There are also many cases of dogs coming to the aid of other dogs. A stray German shepherd who used his body to shield an injured Doberman in a busy Los Angeles intersection was later sold at auction for $1,079.50. "He was sheltering his little mate," said a witness. "He came over and led me to the Doberman and then he went back and lay down and sheltered her again. He put his head right over hers." Both dogs were taken to a nearby animal shelter, where animal regulation officers were unable to save the Doberman, who had suffered severe internal injuries when it was struck by an automobile. They kept the shepherd for seven days in the hope that its owner would retrieve it, but when no one claimed the dog, they held the auction, in which forty people bid the price up to over $1,000.00. The new owner named the dog "Hero."

Alas, there are also dog antiheroes. James Thurber's alcoholic mutt, Barge, was one such canine. When he returned home after a night of carousing to discover that burglars had ransacked the home he had been charged to protect, Barge was so shamed by this violation of his sacred trust that he immediately committed suicide. And then there was Rabchik:

> Who was Rabchik? Where did he come from? That's hard to know. It may be that he was left behind by the former landlord of the yard. It may be that he missed his way, lost his owner, adopted a new one, and stayed on. You know how such things happen: One is taking a walk, and then—there's a lost dog in your tracks. You think, Hey, what's this tagging along? You raise your hand to the dog and shout, "Beat it!" The dog stops, bows like a human, and just as you're trying to smack him one, manages to get even closer. Now you bend; you make a feint with your hand, pretending to throw a rock at him. It does no good. You stand watching the dog; the dog stands watching you. You look silently into each other's eyes. You spit, and start off again. The dog follows, and you're going out of your mind. You grab a stick and go at him fiercely, which gives the dog an idea: He lies down, sticks his feet in the air, trembles and shivers and gazes into your eyes as if to say, "Well, you want to beat me? Beat away."
> That's the kind of dog our Rabchik was.
>
> ■ SHOLEM ALEICHEM,
> "RABCHIK, A JEWISH DOG"

171

MONDO CANINE

And Attila:

He stood up twenty inches high, had a large frame and a forbidding appearance on the whole—but that was all. A variety of people entered the gates of the house every day: mendicants, bill collectors, postmen, tradesmen, and family friends. All of them were warmly received by Attila. The moment the gate clicked, he became alert and stood up looking toward the gate. By the time anyone entered the gate, Attila went blindly charging forward. But that was all. The person had only to stop and smile, and Attila would melt. He would behave as if he apologized for even giving an impression of violence. He would lower his head, curve his body, tuck his tail between his legs, roll his eyes, and moan as if to say, "How sad that you should have mistaken my gesture! I only hurried down to greet you." Till he was patted on the head, stroked, and told that he was forgiven, he would be in extreme misery.

■ R. K. NARAYAN,
"ATTILA"

172

MONDO
CANINE

DOGS AT WAR

Since the dawn of organized warfare, dogs have been used as pack animals, messengers, sentinels, scouts, and mascots. The Gauls used armored dogs with razor-sharp collars to attack Roman cavalry (the collars tore the horses' legs to shreds); the Romans used dogs as messengers (unfortunately, the messages were enclosed in tubes which the dogs were forced to swallow; when the canine messenger arrived at its destination, the dog was disemboweled in order to retrieve the message); Crusaders took dogs to the Holy Land in the belief that they could sniff out infidels; armored dogs accompanied the Spanish in the exploration and conquest of the Americas; and Elizabeth I had an army of a thousand dogs at her service in the war against the Irish rebels.

During the Civil War, Sallie, the bulldog mascot of the Eleventh Pennsylvania Volunteers, regularly went into battle with the troops and tirelessly comforted the wounded. She was wounded herself but recovered after battlefield surgery. When President Lincoln reviewed the Eleventh Pennsylvania with Sallie leading the marching troops, he doffed his hat in her honor. Sallie was subsequently killed in battle and a monument was erected in her honor at Gettysburg.

MONDO CANINE

In World War I trenches, sentinel dogs gave soldiers advance warning of approaching patrols, preventing the enemy from getting close enough to use hand grenades. One such dog, a French canine named Kiki, was wounded in action against an enemy patrol and was evacuated for treatment. He was bandaged and was back at his post within hours, just in time to detect another enemy patrol before it could surprise his unit.

According to Lt. Colonel H. E. Richardson, commandant of the World War I British War Dog School, the qualities necessary in a sentry dog are "acute hearing and scent, sagacity, fidelity, and a strong sense of duty." Although the sentry's mission is less spectacular than many wartime canine functions, it saves the most human life.

Two members of the French war dog service, Za and Helda, had been trained for sentry duty, but when they arrived at the front their commanding officer doubted their ability and refused to put them to work. He was finally persuaded when the two dogs sniffed out a secret enemy outpost 250 meters away. Cabot, another French sentinel dog, intercepted a German messenger dog and "captured" its metal tube containing important enemy dispatches.

During the Great War messenger dogs were used to communicate between the front lines and headquarters because a dog can run faster than a man and presents a smaller target. The World War I messenger dog had a difficult mission. It had to travel great distances, often under fire; it had to overcome obstacles in its path, including rivers and barbed wire fences; and it had to work its way through crowded villages without being distracted by people, cattle, moving vehicles, or civilian dogs.

A British messenger dog named Dick was wounded in action and was evacuated to a field hospital, where his wound was dressed. After a brief convalescence he was returned to the line and resumed his duties carrying messages, but in a few days he grew weaker and began to limp. When further treatment failed to improve his condition, Dick was put to sleep. A post mortem examination revealed a bullet lodged in his chest.

Patsou, a French messenger dog whose infantry company was attacked by the Germans in 1918, ran through a withering barrage, covering 3,000 meters in a little over ten minutes, to deliver a message calling for immediate help. Reinforcements were sent up in time to save what remained of Patsou's unit.

During the siege of Verdun, a small detachment of French troops was cut off from its main force. Short of ammunition and zeroed-in by German artillery, they were on the verge of surrender when Satan, a collie-greyhound mix, was dispatched to the unit carrying two carrier pigeons and a message that reinforcements were on the way. In gas mask and goggles Satan braved intense fire to reach the besieged detachment. He was hit by a bullet but kept going on three legs. He finally reached the French soldiers, and they released the pigeons carrying the coodinates of the German gun position. The pigeons flew back to headquarters, French artillery knocked out the German gun, and the troops were rescued.

An anonymous English setter was with his Algerian master in the trenches during the Battle of the Marne. One night an artillery shell burst nearby, burying the soldier under a mass of earth and debris. The dog immediately began digging for him and continued until his paws were bloody. When he was too weak to dig any more, he began to bark loudly until he attracted the attention of soldiers, who came and rescued the unconscious and seriously wounded man and placed him in an ambulance. The dog followed the ambulance to a field hospital. He was allowed to stay by his master's bedside until he recovered, and the two left the hospital together.

A German shepherd named Tommy was the World War I mascot of a Scottish regiment and always went over the top with his men. He was wounded three times, was gassed when his custom-made gas mask was not put on him in time, was captured, and eventually received the Croix de Guerre for gallantry.

Dogs served on the home front as well. In Britain at least two dogs raised money for various war relief efforts. Brum, a brown spaniel-retriever mix, worked London's Euston Station with a tin cup on his back. He barked to get attention and shook hands whenever someone dropped a coin. And then there was Jack, who had belonged to Edith Cavell, a British nurse who was killed by the Germans in Belgium. After her death he was returned to England and became something of a celebrity, making numerous personal appearances and posing for photographs which were sold to benefit the Red Cross.

MONDO
CANINE

> [An] Airedale . . . knocked a young German boy from harm's way as a grenade exploded in Berlin during the last days of the Second World War—the very same dog whose bright eyes and bearded mug persuaded an occupying Russian garrison to breach military regulations and provide a pot of goulash, which sustained the Airedale and the boy's family. ■ CHIP BROWN

America's dogs answered the call to arms and served their country as sentinels, scouts, messengers, and pack animals. The most decorated U.S. dog during World War II was Chips, a collie-husky-German shepherd mix. After serving in North Africa as a guard dog, Chips participated in the invasion of Sicily and won a Silver Star for capturing a machine gun nest.

Daisy, the mascot of a Norwegian merchant ship torpedoed in the North Atlantic, went into the icy sea with the surviving crewmen and throughout the night swam from man to man, licking their faces and giving them comfort and encouragement until

they were rescued the following morning.

And La Cloche, a white Labrador, shipped out with her owner, a French merchant seaman who couldn't swim. When the ship was torpedoed, La Cloche held her master's head above water until they were rescued.

At the end of the war, surviving members of the K-9 Corps received honorable discharges and were demobilized, rehabilitated, and sent home to their prewar families. One dog who had been in the service for the duration rushed into the house, hastily greeted his former family, dashed into the yard, and dug up a bone he had buried five years earlier.

This poster began appearing soon after the United States entered World War II. ▶

A Message To
America's Dog-Owners

TOTAL WAR has made it necessary to call to the colors many of the nation's dogs. Thousands of dogs, donated by patriotic men, women and children and trained for special duties with the Armed Forces, are serving on all fronts as well as standing guard against saboteurs at home.

More thousands of dogs are needed. New recruits are being inducted daily at the War Dog Training Centers, rushed into training courses which skill them as sentries, message carriers, airplane spotters, pack-carriers—and other tasks which must remain secret. The Army, Navy, Coast Guard and Marines depend on the generosity of the dog owners of the United States to keep that stream of recruits at full flood. They depend on those who own no dogs to speed news of this need to every corner of the land.

Most wanted are dogs of the larger breeds—Belgian Shepherds, Boxers, Airedales, German Shepherds, Doberman Pinschers, Dalmatians, German Short Haired Pointers, Collies, Standard Poodles, Eskimos, Siberian Huskies, St. Bernards, Irish Water Spaniels, Labrador Retrievers, and a dozen others. They must be at least a year old, not more than five. Weight and height requirements vary, according to breed, from 50 pounds to 125 pounds. The animals must be temperamentally suited to military tasks— not gun-shy, not storm-shy. Perfect physical condition is essential.

To register a dog for duty, to learn how to help in the campaign to build up this new unit of the country's military might, communicate at once with the national headquarters of the official dog procurement agency:

DOGS FOR DEFENSE, Inc.
22 EAST 60th STREET, NEW YORK CITY

MY DOG

My Alsatian Tito . . . knew, by "telepathy," exactly which people got on my nerves, and when. Nothing could prevent her from biting, gently but surely, all such people on their posteriors.

■ KONRAD LORENZ,
KING SOLOMON'S RING

Near this spot
Are deposited the remains of one
Who possessed Beauty without Vanity,
Strength without Indolence,
Courage without Ferocity,
And all the virtues of Man, without his vices.
This praise, which would be unmeaning Flattery
If inscribed over human ashes,
Is but a just tribute to the Memory of
BOATSWAIN, a Dog.

■ LORD BYRON,
*INSCRIPTION ON THE TOMB
OF HIS NEWFOUNDLAND DOG,
1808*

Yet always, even in his most cosseted and idle days, he managed to preserve the grave preoccupation of one professionally concerned with retrieving things that smell; and consoled himself with pastimes such as cricket, which he played in a manner highly specialized, following the ball up the moment it left the bowler's hand, and sometimes retrieving it before it reached the batsman. When remonstrated with, he would consider a little, hanging out a pink tongue and looking rather too eagerly at the ball, then canter slowly out to a sort of forward short leg. Why he always chose that particular position it is difficult to say; possibly he could lurk there better than anywhere else, the batsman's eye not being on him, and the bowler's not too much. As a fieldsman he was perfect, but for an occasional belief that he was not merely short leg, but slip, point, mid-off, and wicket-keep; and perhaps a tendency to make the ball a little "jubey." But he worked tremendously, watching every movement; for he knew the game thoroughly, and seldom delayed it more than three minutes when he secured the ball. And if that ball were really lost, then indeed he took over the proceedings with an intensity and quiet vigor that destroyed many shrubs, and the solemn satisfaction which comes from being in the very center of the stage. ■ JOHN GALSWORTHY, *"MEMORIES"*

The emotional calendar of my life is the names of my dogs—Daisy, the Springer Spaniel of my childhood; Gretel, the Boxer of my boyhood; Molly, the English Pointer of my college years; and the long string of bird dogs: Jesse, Patrick, Pepper, Babe, K.D., Sadie and Reba that have gotten me to age fifty. I'd be happy to have my biography be the stories of my dogs. To me, to live without dogs would mean accepting a form of blindness. ■ THOMAS McGUANE

The dog was the greatest dog in the world. Cairn terrier, one of those little dogs. My mother's dog. He was one of these dogs that will play fetch forever. And he just loved to go for walks. I would take him for walks to Evanston, about a fifteen-mile walk. His feet would be sore, but he would love it. ■ BILL MURRAY

Our dog Polo is our third Cavalier King Charles Spaniel. When my wife and I were married in 1971, we felt the family deserved a dog; and her son Peter, then six years old, after poring over a book of dog pictures, decided we must have a King Charles Spaniel. It took a little trouble to find one, but we finally succeeded. Peter named him Sinbad, and we all adored him. Then one day, running in Central Park without a leash, Sinbad dashed into a roadway, and a taxi killed him.

To alleviate the grief we then acquired Molly of the same breed. Peter and our new son Robert, then about five, thought that Molly as a lady should have progeny; so we mated her with Blenheim, Lauren Bacall's beloved King Charles Spaniel. After several unproductive weekends together at a hospitable kennel, Molly finally became pregnant. In the summer of 1980 she gave birth to two small puppies. Robert promptly named them Marco and Polo. Since Blenheim was the father, Lauren Bacall had the choice of the litter, and she took Marco. Polo, now nearly ten years old, is not so frisky as he was, but he still brightens our lives every day. ■ ARTHUR SCHLESINGER, JR.

Mickey . . . had been accustomed to be in the dining room with the other people. He didn't get in the way; for his own peace of mind he always stayed in the safety zone inside the stretchers of the serving table. A cat claws and miaows when you eat, but a dog who has not been spoiled lies down at some distance and looks tactfully away, pretending you are not eating so you will not be embarrassed by a sense of your selfishness. It was not the food that attracted Mickey, but the sociability. If man can be classified as a social animal, so can dogs. Mickey, even when asleep or seeming so, would dreamily thump his tail when happy laughter burst out.

■ BERTHA DAMON,
"RUFFLED PAWS"

MONDO
CANINE

As I lay on the floor in the dark, empty room, Tuppins, my puppy, licked at the tears running down my face. "Oh, Tuppins," I sobbed, "Why has God forsaken me?"

■ TAMMY FAYE BAKKER

My dog is half pit bull, half poodle. Not much of a guard dog, but a vicious gossip.

■ CRAIG SHOEMAKER

A spaniel, Beau, that fares like you,
   Well fed, and at his ease,
Should wiser be than to pursue
   Each trifle that he sees . . .
My dog! What remedy remains,
   Since, teach you all I can,
I see you, after all my pains,
   So much resemble man!

■ WILLIAM COWPER,
"BEAU"

Puli, my dog (he is a puli and his name is Puli and it wasn't my idea), is so wonderful. In the eleven years we have had him we have always called him to dinner in the same way (briefly—"Dinner, Puli") and yet every day he turns his head in sheer wonderment and happiness for a few moments before dashing to it, not quite believing that he is really getting dinner again tonight. He may be a dog, but don't tell me he doesn't have a real grip on life.

■ KENDALL HAILEY,
THE DAY I BECAME AN AUTODIDACT

My [Dalmation] Chili, first of all, must never know that he was named for a lady. In the late 1940's a Hollywood film actress burst upon the

181

scene calling herself Chili Williams. Miss Williams' press agents had decreed that as a publicity stunt she would wear only polka dots. Whenever I see a Dalmation, I think of her and Hollywood and all the crazy stunts they used to employ out there to publicize newcomers and hopefuls. My dog Chili is highly photogenic, loves the camera, and, for all I know, probably thinks he's a movie star as well.

■ BOBBY SHORT

You didn't have to throw a stick in the water to get him to go in. Of course, he would bring back a stick if you did throw one in. He would even have brought back a piano if you had thrown one in.

■ JAMES THURBER,
"SNAPSHOT OF A DOG"

When my older brother was thirteen—that would have made me about eight and a half—Peter arrived. He was an English cocker spaniel, all black with reddish-brown markings, perfectly balanced accents over the eyes, on the cheeks, and on the legs. He was a magnificent animal and was so close to human it was frightening. We moved from the country town of Methuen, Massachusetts, to Boston while we had Peter, and I remember the day he was hit by a car as he rushed off our apartment-house lawn to greet me coming home from school. He ran back onto the grass and promptly vomited. Our family pediatrician was coming that day, and he examined Peter's leg and splinted it. It probably wasn't even broken. As long as Peter lived—and that was to a ripe old age, approaching fifteen, as I recall—he would begin limping the moment he was scolded or thought he was about to be. Otherwise, his leg was fine. He never forgot the sympathy he had gotten while splinted, and although I can't determine with exactitude what intelligence is needed to develop a ruse like a fake limp, it seems to me it must be considerable.

183

I suppose it is always possible that it wasn't intelligence but something rather more Pavlovian than that. Still, I like to think he was a very clever dog. ◾ ROGER CARAS,
A CELEBRATION OF DOGS

There used to be a special breed of fox terrier popular in Russia, employed on bear-hunting expeditions. Being very small and very courageous, they would contrive to get behind the bear, when sheltering in his cave, and by biting at his heels drive him out. Some friends . . . made me a present of one of these dogs. He was eleven weeks old at the time, but grew up to be quite the smallest and quite the fiercest animal I have ever lived with. His name—I forget the Russian for it—signified "Seven Devils," but for short I called him Peter. . . . He was an affectionate little beggar, in his cranky way. He would sit on my desk as I worked; and would never go to sleep unless he was lying on something belonging to one or another of us. One of the girls' hats would do as well as anything. He would take it on to a chair and curl himself inside it; and his one answer to all their storming and raving was: "What I have, I hold; what I take, I keep." Well, it taught them not to leave their things about. He would keep close enough to me in the country; but the town always confused him; and often I would lose him. He would make no attempt to find me, but would just sit down in the middle of the street where he had last noticed me, and howl. In Munich, he came to be known as "The English dog that for his master screams." Policemen would knock at my door to inform me that he was screaming in such and such a street; and that I must come immediately and fetch him home. ◾ JEROME K. JEROME,
MY LIFE AND TIMES

In pitchy darkness, the river roaring in my ears, I turn into the poplar avenue, and after the first few steps I am enveloped in a soundless storm

184

MONDO
CANINE

of prancings and swishings; on the first occasion I did not know what was happening. "Bashan?" I inquired into the blackness. The prancings and swishings redouble—is this a dancing dervish or a Berserk warrior here on my path? But not a sound; and directly I stand still, I feel those honest, wet and muddy paws on the lapels of my raincoat, and a snapping and flapping in my face . . . as I stoop down to pat the lean shoulder, equally wet with snow or rain. Yes, the good soul has come to meet the train. Well informed as always upon my comings and goings, he has got up at what he judged to be the right time, to fetch me from the station. He may have been waiting a long while, in snow or rain, yet his joy at my final appearance knows no resentment at my faith-lessness, though I have neglected him all day and brought his hopes to naught.
■ THOMAS MANN,
"BASHAN"

The greatest dog I ever had was a Golden Retriever named Charlie. After he was gone, like a lot of dog lovers, I said, "No way, never again, another dog to love and lose." Then one day my wife came home with this little white fluffy thing with big black eyes. She said it was a Bichon Frise. It took a while and another one before I "fell" all over again, and harder than ever. We named our two Bichons "Char-donay" and "Chablis," and like truly fine wines, they grow more val-uable to us with each passing day. They are also really loud, pesky, and impossible to house break. But we love them anyway and highly recommend the Bichon "experience."
■ FRANK GIFFORD

My dog can bark like a congressman, fetch like an aide, beg like a press secretary and play dead like a receptionist when the phone rings.
■ CONGRESSMAN GERALD SOLOMON
(R-NEW YORK)

As soon as I arrive at the house, [my Cardigan Welsh Corgi] Laurie starts running, hits my chest, knocks me down, and licks my face. It's become a family ritual. ■ BEVERLY SILLS

Scott, the Border collie, is the brightest but not the deepest of the two pets. His herding instinct is so strong that he confuses tractors on a baseball field for sheep. He was hospitalized twice. Once by a line drive and once for attacking a tractor tread. [Taxi, the Labrador retriever] likes to take strolls by himself and believes dogcatchers are friendly innkeepers who'll take care of a meal. He's gullible and has never learned to fight back against a ruthless world.
■ TOM HAYDEN

It is fatal to let any dog know that he is funny, for he immediately loses his head and starts hamming it up. As an instance of this I would point to Rudolph, a dachshund I once owned, whose slogan was Anything for a Laugh. Dachshunds are always the worst offenders in this respect because of their peculiar shape. It is only natural that when a dog finds that his mere appearance makes the viewing public giggle, he should assume that Nature intended him for a comedian's role.

I had a cottage at the time outside an English village, not far from a farm where they kept ducks, and one day the farmer called on me to say his ducks were disappearing and suspicion had fallen on my Rudolph. Why? I asked, and he said because mine was the only dog in the vicinity except his own Towser, and Towser had been so carefully trained that he would not touch a duck if you brought it to him with orange sauce over it.

I was indignant. I said he had only to gaze into Rudolph's candid brown eyes to see how baseless were his suspicions. Had he not, I asked, heard of foxes? Or weasels? Or stoats? How much more likely that one of these was the Bad Guy in the sequence? He was beginning to waver and seemed on the verge of an apology, when Rudolph, who had been listening with the greatest of interest and at a certain point had left the room, came trotting in with a duck in his mouth.

■ P. G. WODEHOUSE

Shag . . . was too great a gentleman to take part in the plebeian work of killing rats for which he was originally needed, but he certainly added, we felt, to the respectability of the family. He seldom went for a walk without punishing the impertinence of middle-class dogs who neglected the homage due to his rank, and we had to enclose the royal jaws in a muzzle long after that restriction was legally unnecessary. As he advanced in middle life he became certainly rather autocratic, not only with his own kind, but with us, his masters and mistresses; such a title though was absurd where Shag was concerned, so we called ourselves his uncles and aunts. The solitary occasion when he found it necessary to inflict marks of his displeasure on human flesh was once when a visitor rashly tried to treat him as an ordinary pet-dog and tempted him with sugar and called him "out of his name" by the contemptible lap-dog title of "Fido." Then Shag, with characteristic independence, refused the sugar and took a satisfactory mouthful of calf instead. But when he felt he was treated with due respect he was the most faithful of friends.

■ VIRGINIA WOOLF,
"ON A FAITHFUL FRIEND"

Most dogs love car riding, but to [my beagle] Sam it was a passion that never waned—even in the night hours. He would gently leave his basket when the world was asleep . . . and follow me out into the cold. He would be on the seat before I got the car door fully open.

■ JAMES HERRIOT,
"VET IN HARNESS"

MONDO
CANINE

[My boxer] Gangster is the truest friend I can ever ask for.
■ SYLVESTER STALLONE

He's a worker. He's a lover. He's my children.
■ ANNIE McNIFF-BURGESS,
ON HER DOG TISBET

When I was elected Majority Leader of the Senate in 1984, my wife Elizabeth presented me with a very special gift—a Schnauzer puppy named Leader. Elizabeth adopted him from a local shelter, and it is one of the best presents I've ever had.

We try to bring Leader to the office when we can, but that can be a real challenge. My office in the U.S. Capitol, for instance, has a lot of people traffic and a lot of doors. In other words, plenty of opportunity for a dog to take a stroll at his convenience. One time Leader strolled into the busy hallways and was gone for about half an hour. Finally, a guard called to tell us Leader was loose in the Capitol Rotunda. That ended our dog's free reign in the halls of Congress.

They say that dogs often take on the characteristics of their owners, and I must admit, Leader and I have quite a few similarities. We've both called press conferences (this is true), we're both intensely loyal, and we both bark at liberals from time to time.
■ SENATOR ROBERT DOLE
(R-KANSAS)

Ah! you should keep dogs—fine animals—sagacious creatures—dog of my own once—Pointer—surprising instinct—out shooting one day—entering inclosure—whistled—dog stopped—whistled again—Ponto—no go: stock still—called him—Ponto, Ponto—wouldn't move—dog transfixed—staring at a board—looked up, saw an inscription—

"Gamekeeper has orders to shoot all dogs found in this inclosure"—wouldn't pass it—wonderful dog—valuable dog that—very.

■ CHARLES DICKENS,
THE PICKWICK PAPERS

I was lying on my side chewing a grass stem, and Jock lay down in front of me about a meter away. It was a habit of his. He liked to watch my face, and often when I rolled over to ease one side and lie on the other he would get up and come round deliberately to the other side and sling himself down in front of me again. There he would lie with his hind legs sprawled on one side, his front legs straight out, and his head resting on his paws. He would lie like that without a move, his little dark eyes fixed on mine and he would blink and blink, like a drowsy child, fighting against sleep until it beat him.

■ PERCY FITZPATRICK,
JOCK OF THE BUSHVELD

189

When they play, they're like a vaudeville act. When I toss a tennis ball into the pool, Max [a mixed breed] sits on the edge and supervises Jennifer [a German shepherd], who dives in for the ball. She then gives the ball to Max, who proudly presents it to us.

■ SIDNEY SHELDON

Stan was an excellent ball player. Whereas Bob used to play "Catch the ball and eat it," Stan preferred "Double dog ball," in which two balls are put into play at all times, the one in the mouth being released at the same time that the one in the hand hits the air. The game could go on indefinitely—in fact, the more indefinitely, the better. And because he was so enthusiastic in his playing, I generally chose to overlook the fact that he almost always took a dump on the dog ball field, during the third inning, with the ball still in his mouth. Anyone who has ever played this game will tell you that ordinarily this is an automatic out.

■ MERRILL MARKOE

He was born in Bercy on the outskirts of Paris and trained in France, and while he knows a little poodle-English, he responds quickly only to commands in French. Otherwise he has to translate, and that slows him down. He is a very big poodle, of a color called *bleu*, and he is blue when he is clean. Charley is a born diplomat. He prefers negotiation to fighting, and properly so, since he is very bad at fighting. Only once in his ten years has he been in trouble—when he met a dog who refused to negotiate. Charley lost a piece of this right ear that time. But he is a good watch dog—has a roar like a lion, designed to conceal from night-wandering strangers the fact that he couldn't bite his way out of a *cornet du papier*. He is a good friend and traveling companion, and would rather travel about than anything he can imagine.

■ JOHN STEINBECK,
TRAVELS WITH CHARLEY

My dogs don't travel by boat. And they don't go with me to Paris, London or New York. But they do go with me to Gstaad and Capri.

■ VALENTINO

From the very beginning Cooper loved the water and went in it all the time. Often, I'd come home from class and whistle for him if he wasn't on the front porch. In a couple of minutes he'd come running out from the trees, his wet fur covered with dripping green algae. He'd been lounging in the creek, lying in a pool he even cleared of a few rocks himself.

He would be smiling as always. "Peter, what do you want me to do now?" he seemed to say. I'd motion him to come home with me, down a hill, past a bank, and over to a delivery dock where there was a big hose, and I'd wash all the creek slime off him. Once Cooper, fresh from the creek, tracked me into an art class, walked right up to the naked young woman who was our model, lay down on her feet—and became part of the drawing. He moved even less than she did. He may have been wet, but he sure knew he was handsome.

■ PETER JENKINS,
CLOSE FRIENDS

I've always loved dogs, but I never had one as a boy because our house was too small. When I was a cop, I never took stray dogs to the pound, because animal shelters do 'em in. Instead, I found homes for all of them. It breaks my heart to see stray dogs. . . . Casey is a member of our family . . . except when he's been bad; then he's mine. I punish him by saying, "Bad dog," which our parrot, Andy, likes to mimic. I don't believe in using physical force on dogs.

■ FRANK RIZZO

191

I clearly remember my Alsatian, Argus, choosing a wife and going off with her to our orchard and digging a fifteen-foot underground passage and bedroom at the end for her to have her litter in; his other wives were just for business purposes only, this was the one true mate. We allowed her to have her nine puppies down there, and seeing Argus standing erect on top of the entrance the day the mother whelped was a thrilling sight, for we felt the true nature of the dogs had been allowed to develop by choosing their own home and bringing up the babies in a homely atmosphere.

Only when the babies were fourteen days old and near to weaning time did we interfere. They were the most wonderful litter we had ever bred. I had never met before with instinct like that and I have never since. When we opened up the nest we saw that it was beautifully made around a corner of the passage, with straw and hay the bitch had picked up in her mouth, plus masses of her own hair she had plucked from her chest. The nest was scrupulously clean and dry; in fact, she was a model housekeeper, one that many human mothers could well emulate.

■ BARBARA WOODHOUSE,
NO BAD DOGS

The one single moment that comes closest to summing up my friendship with Juno—and the whole reason for liking dogs—took place not far from my home at the time, on those cliffs on the west side of the Hudson River. Juno and I had been hiking strenuously, and we were taking a rest. We were sitting on a rock, looking out over the river, toward Westchester County. It was a perfect spring day, gold and blue and green. We felt good.

After a while, I began to realize that the dog and I were sharing a thought. It wasn't anything very special or complicated—it was something a man could think, and a dog could think. It was just something like . . . "Ahh!"

■ DANIEL PINKWATER,
"LIFE WITH JUNO"

A small dog of ours, a sort of terrier, is able to distinguish a particular tune. I happened to play the tune for some time, and he was at first taught to dance it, receiving a piece of bread as a reward, but now he seems to enjoy the pleasure of keeping time to the music with his little hind paws, while he licks the hands of the person holding him. He often lies apparently asleep in the room while I play anything else, but at the first notes of *his* tune, he pricks up his ears and begs to be held up to dance. The same result has often happened when he has been asleep in a distant part of the house. Sometimes when I sit down to the piano and do not play his *morceau*, he whines until I indulge him.

■ "W.R.,"
LETTER TO "THE LEISURE HOUR" (1874)

I firmly believe that some dogs can read minds. Dixie, my Labrador, usually joins me at breakfast, and I usually give her a scrap of toast or bacon. I have often noticed that when I *decide* to choose a scrap for her, and well before I pick it up, she will trot to my side and stand, waiting. She must have read my mind. There's no other plausible explanation.　■ J. BRYAN, III,
HODGEPODGE II

When I was a bird-hunting boy, my first dog sustained a broken leg under what might be termed compromising circumstances. Detected in the act of embezzling a turkey drumstick from the kitchen table, he departed via the nearest window, his exit being accelerated by a fusillade of brooms wielded by the irate womenfolk. Buck stood not on the order of his going but departed with such precipitancy that his parachute forgot to open.

For several weeks I showered attention on the invalid, with the result that when the leg mended he was, as my mother said, "spoiled rotten." Thereafter when he wanted something or wanted to get out of something, he limped his way to success. But it didn't occur to me that he was feigning until the hunting season opened.

I soon observed that whenever I ordered him across the creek or into a brier patch, he invariably began to limp, *but on the wrong foot.* The old malingerer had forgotten which leg he had broken, but it was too good a racket to abandon. The sight of me cutting a switch, however, possessed such remarkable curative powers that he promptly addressed himself to the business at hand.　■ HAVILAH BABCOCK,
"LIARS SHOULD HAVE GOOD MEMORIES"

193

Our Lab, Boomer, is a nice, sweet, loving girl just like me, and her sister, Tasha [a Yorkshire terrier], is a grouchy, spoiled rotten little girl just like my sisters, Louise and Irene.
■ BARBARA MANDRELL

Bill . . . never achieved anything. Never did he sit with the golden lumps on his nose, he ate them at once. Never did he stay to heel. Never did he remember what he was supposed to do with his paw when one of us offered him a hand. The truth was, I understood then, watching the training sessions, that Bill was stupid.

■ DORIS LESSING,
"THE STORY OF TWO DOGS"

Helen has a nice smile. McGuire is a big dog. He's easygoing and always up for anything. And he'll eat anything you drop on the floor. Harry used to sneeze on command, but then he went deaf. As for their personalities, well, none of them are like me. I mean, I can't see any of them writing a column.   ■ PETE DEXTER

It was then that the dog came back. We heard him calling out before we saw him, his huge woof-woof "My name is Duke! My name is Duke! I'm your dog! I'm your dog!" Then we saw him streaking through the trees, through the park space of oaks and maples between our house and the post gate. Later the MPs would say that he stopped and wagged his tail at them before he passed through the gate, as if he understood that he should be stopping to show his ID card. He ran to us, bounding across the crusted, glass-like snow—ran into the history of our family, all the stories we would tell about him after he was dead. Years and years later, whenever we came back together at the family table, we would start the dog stories. He was the dog who caught the live fish with his mouth, the one who stole a pound of butter off the commissary loading dock and brought it to us in his soft bird dog's mouth without a tooth mark on the package. He was the dog who broke out of Charley Battery the morning of an ice storm, traveled fourteen miles across the needled grasses of frozen pastures, through the prickly frozen mud of

MONDO
CANINE

orchards, across backyard fences in small towns, and found the lost family.

■ STEPHANIE VAUGHN,
"DOG HEAVEN"

Jet was a workaholic in the field . . . loved goose hunting on the Eastern Shore and had the drive of a springer on upland birds. But besides that, what a gentleman he was in public! I have to smile when I think of the time we were invited to be a part of a convention in Philadelphia. Booked at the headquarters, the elegant Bellevue Stratford hotel, where no dogs were allowed, I put on black glasses and lived for four days in the hotel as a blind man. It wasn't easy, and in my absentminded way nearly a disaster. Example: I fogot and left my reading glasses hanging on the string around my neck, while fumbling in public in my black "blind man" glasses. It took me time to learn how to play my role, but not Jet. He carried off his end of the deal with style, leading me everywhere, up and down steps, around revolving doors, even into the dining room. The doorman gave him a pat every morning and remarked how well trained he was to do his job.

■ RICHARD A. WOLTERS,
GAME DOG

195

Strange was the only dog I've ever known who could belch at will. It was his idea of high comedy. If my mother had some of her friends over for a game of pinochle, Strange would slip into the house and slouch over to the ladies. Then he would emit a loud belch. Apparently, he mistook shudders of revulsion for a form of applause, because he would sit there on his haunches, grinning modestly up at the group and preparing an encore. "Stop, stop!" he would snarl, as I dragged him back outdoors. "They love me! They'll die laughing at my other routine! It'll have them on the floor!" I will not speak here of his other routine.

In general appearance, Strange could easily have been mistaken for

MONDO CANINE

your average brown-and-white mongrel with floppy ears and a shaggy tail, except that depravity was written all over him. He looked as if he sold dirty postcards to support an opium habit.

■ PATRICK F. McMANUS,
"SKUNK DOG"

One spring day Bonnie, my Cairn terrier, saw a woodchuck disappear down a hole in our barn floor. Every day after that, for six months, Bonnie "commuted" out to the barn and sat beside the hole, watching intently and occasionally whimpering. As the days lengthened into summer, so did her work hours. We brought her food and water out next to the hole, and she returned to the house only after dark, to sleep and dream of a woodchuck she would have been very sorry to actually catch.

Bonnie later died, hairless and smelly but still feisty, after eating an entire package of caramel candies that glued her jaw shut and gave her a heart attack.

■ C.E. CRIMMINS

Never have I experienced a serenity and sweetness of disposition as with my Chocolate Lab.

■ MORTIMER B. ZUCKERMAN

I can still see my first dog in all the moods and situations that memory has filed him away in; for six years he met me at the same place after school and convoyed me home—a service he thought up himself. A boy doesn't forget that sort of association.

■ E.B. WHITE,
"THE CARE AND TRAINING OF A DOG"

For a number of years past I have been agreeably encumbered by a very large and dissolute dachshund named Fred. Of all the dogs whom I have served I've never known one who understood so much of what I say or held it in such deep contempt. When I address Fred I never have

to raise either my voice or my hopes. He even disobeys me when I instruct him in something that he wants to do. And when I answer his peremptory scratch at the door and hold the door open for him to walk through, he stops in the middle and lights a cigarette, just to hold me up.
■ E.B. WHITE,
"DOG TRAINING"

I have had dogs all my life and I have learned that they are as different from one another as people are, but I have never had a dog like Fafner. A golden red-brown dachshund, he was named after Wagner's dragon because of his dragon-shaped paws and long, thin body. Fafner was a dog of dogs, an old soul with extrasensory perception, always on the verge of crossing over from dogdom to personhood. He would sit up on his hind legs and look me in the eye to sense my mood. If I was gay, he would play the clown, tossing his blanket in the air or pushing his ball with his nose. If I was sad, he would bury his head under my arm or give my cheek a furtive lick. He knew so many words that my husband and I took to spelling in front of him. Of course, always being treated as a person (he often sat at the table with a napkin around his neck), Fafner considered himself a person. His attitude toward other dogs was a mixture of arrogance and contempt, and he barked furiously whenever he saw one. He detested the whole canine race.
■ BROOKE ASTOR,
"OUR FRIEND FAFNER"

My pugs, Bess and Stella, are my idols. They have the greatest sense of entitlement of any creatures I have ever known. They do nothing all day and feel no guilt about their sloth. They do not protect me, they do not console me when I am blue, they care only for their own comfort. For example, if you put them in a room with nothing but two socks in it, they'll push the socks together and make themselves a bed. Other than that, they have only one other skill—begging!—which they've

197

MONDO CANINE

elevated to an art form. My pugs are shameless in their greed, they will hound me relentlessly with an entire repertoire of noises—including hellish yipping, pathetic whimpering, and blood-freezing squeals—until I give them what they want.

With these skills I could conquer the world.

■ MARGO KAUFMAN

My dog, Reggie, likes to watch television for hours at a stretch. When we're eating dinner in the kitchen he goes into the den and barks until I turn the set on for him. When he sees animals on the screen he goes bananas. He follows them when they move and when they go off the screen he walks around the side of the TV to see where they went. He especially likes "Hunter" and the cartoons on Saturday morning. I hope he doesn't ruin his eyes. ■ IRV LANDER

198

The only dog I ever knew which died of a broken heart was an Irish terrier male that we had to send away from us one winter that we spent in apartments. Poor Badger, shall I ever forget the deep trouble in your hazel eyes, as we put you into the crate? And yet you trusted us, sat quietly while the slats were being hammered into place, went away without outcry.

And there was another male, a cocker spaniel, that we gave away when we were moving a distance. I was a child then, but I remember how my heart ached when I heard that he had gone to our empty house every day, sat down before the door, raised his muzzle toward heaven and uttered a howl full of sorrow, as of the end of the world. He would then go to the station, from whence we had left, and walk with sad dignity up and down the platform. One day my father returned to the town on business, and the spaniel saw his figure in the doorway of a carriage, as the train drew out. He ran after the train, faster and faster as it increased its speed, his long feathered ears flying, his eyes full of anguish. I have heard my father say that he seldom had been so moved as when he saw the spaniel's strength failing. He could not endure it. He pulled the bell-cord of the train and stopped it. He alighted and gathered the spaniel into his arms. How he managed to convince the authorities that it was necessary to stop the train, I do not know.

■ MAZO DE LA ROCHE,
PORTRAIT OF A DOG

By human standards, Jason was a huge success professionally. He was servile to the point of embarrassment, and was incapable of looking anyone in the eye for more than a few seconds, with the exception of insects. He frequently licked babies, and only an hour before he died he assiduously marked the trunk of a maple tree.

He was well known for his guilty expression, and on those occasions when he rifled through the garbage it was not uncommon for him to look as though he deserved the death penalty.

■ ANNA QUINDLEN

199

I knew . . . a German shepherd who grumbled noisily at the other dogs when they didn't obey—a female, as it happens. My Airedale was another matter. When, in training him to retrieve, I began placing the dumbbell in odd ways, he enjoyed the play on form. At one point, for instance, I set the dumbbell on its end for the fun of it, and he scooped it up happily, tossing it in the air a few times on his way back with it, to show his appreciation of the joke. A very fine, very serious German shepherd I worked with, confronted with the same situation, glared disapprovingly at the dumbbell and at me, then pushed it carefully back into its proper position before picking it up and returning with it, rather sullenly. The Airedale's enjoyment of oddity and ingenuity made him a good candidate for movie work, whereas the shepherd is better suited for something like tracking.

■ VICKI HEARNE,
ADAM'S TASK

We believe very strongly that you need two dogs. We have Earnest, our large main dog, and Zippy, our small emergency back-up dog, 'cause you never know when a dog is going to go down. In fact, at one point we had both dogs go down briefly. What happened was Zippy reached puberty and started hitting on Earnest, which was very funny because Zippy is the size of a mature cockroach and Earnest is the size of a dump truck. It wasn't going to work out, but Zippy didn't know that. He just kept trying and trying, so we decided to take him in and get the volume turned way down on the stereo system of his manhood, if you know what I'm saying.

At the same time, Earnest developed some kind of a cyst in her paw. We took them both in and brought them both back and they were two hurtin' cowpokes. Zippy had one of those collars they put around dogs' heads so they can't get at themselves, like a satellite dish. And Earnest had a bag on her foot. The two of them were pathetic: Zippy could barely move without banging his radar dish on the floor, and Earnest *thought* she could move, but every third or fourth step she would slip and almost fall. She'd go *step . . . step . . . step . . . slip . . . step . . . step . . . step . . . slip.* They'd be at one end of the house and someone would come to the door and you'd hear this barking and howling back there—the two dogs attempting to get to the front door to kill the person, which is their job, you know. There'd be about five minutes of *step . . . step . . . step . . . slip,* and the banging of the satellite dish. Finally, they'd come around the corner, two pathetic,

200

wretched animals, and of course if it really was a burglar, he would have removed by that point all the major appliances.

But they're great. I have them with me every day. When I go out back to work in my office, I ask, "Do you want to go to work?" And they know what that means. All three of us go out the back door and walk to my office, and they stay with me all day. This has been going on for years now. But neither one of them has ever had an idea. Not one single idea.　　　　　■ DAVE BARRY

ARNOLD!

DANIEL PINKWATER

 Selling us Arnold, our second Alaskan malamute, was Larry Porketta's masterpiece. Only selling a dog already dead, or made of acrylic, would have been more of a coup.

"This pup is special," Larry said.

"He looks sort of scuzzy," I said.

"He's six months old. It's an awkward age for malamutes. That's why I'm prepared to let him go for a pittance."

"He's sort of runty and scrawny, isn't he?"

"Not at all. In fact, he's big for his size. Here, feel of him."

He thrust the puppy into my arms. It licked my face. Jill reached over to hug the puppy and got kissed too.

We were goners. We took Arnold with us.

When we got him home and looked at him in a good light, we could see that his head was too big for his body, his tail appeared to be screwed on wrong, and he had a tendency to bump into things.

There was nothing right with Arnold! Half his weight was intestinal worms. He had a bad cough. His feet stank, and he would have a fit if he heard a sudden noise.

In time, Arnold calmed down a bit. He didn't hit the ceiling whenever a truck rolled by. He grew into proportion and got to be downright handsome. He also began to exhibit a sort of charm and . . . well . . . suavity and elegance.

But he also began to show a side we never dreamed he had. He turned into a fighter. He didn't fight with Juno, our first malamute. She had wisely begun to intimidate him from the first day—and he never lost his respect for her quick tooth.

Arnold's potential opponents—actually his victims—were all dogs on earth, other than Juno.

Our best guess is that during the six months Arnold had lived before we got him he'd been abused in various ways by humans and dogs. Now he was evening the score.

Malamutes were bred to pull freight. It's not unheard of for them to move a ton in weight-pulling contests. If Arnold saw a German shepherd he wanted to destroy while being walked on a leash, it took some doing to keep it from happening.

We must have read a hundred books about dog training.

I consulted numerous experts. Some of these people were remarkable. They had brilliant theories about how Arnold got to be so antisocial. None of them had any useful suggestions about how to turn him around.

One trainer suggested a method. First, we'd have to find another aggressive malamute, whose owner wanted to cure him. Then we'd muzzle the two of them so they couldn't harm one another, tie them together by the collar with a cord two feet long, and throw them into a closet for an hour or so. This way they'd get it out of their system, the trainer explained. They'd try to fight, get frustrated, fall asleep, wake up, try again, and so forth, until they were sick of the whole business.

We tried it.

All that happened was that Arnold learned how to menace another dog while taking a nap. When I peeked into the closet, Arnold was fast asleep, growling loudly, and the other malamute was crying for its mother.

Next we simply enrolled Arnold in an ordinary dog obedience class—the kind they have at the local VFW or adult ed program. We warned the instructor, of course, and Arnold wore his muzzle to class.

MONDO
CANINE

These classes are usually held in some gymnasium or similar space—and they're a little like a square dance. The instructor stands in the middle of the room, calling out commands, and the trainees and dogs march around, doing his bidding.

At first I simply dragged Arnold around the floor. He'd travel on his back or side much of the time, pawing the air and screaming threats at the other dogs. Occasionally, he'd grovel and paw his way toward some terrified poodle—and I'd drag him away.

Each course lasted six or eight weeks. Arnold went through six courses—all identical, all beginners' obedience. By the third course, I was able to dispense with the muzzle.

Arnold continued vocalizing, but I had become so strong and expert in handling the leash that I could control his occasional lunges at some innocent beagle.

Juno, mostly from just watching week after week, had become a sort of obedience genius, and we'd take her out and win trophies with her on weekends.

A full two years after I'd started trying to train Arnold, I took him to an obedience match sponsored by the local malamute club. It was an all-northern dog match—Siberian huskies, malamutes, Samoyeds and Akitas—all of them feisty and scrappy by nature. The match was held indoors—space was limited—and Arnold brushed up against a number of tough customers.

Arnold never raised a lip to any of them—even though he had several explicit invitations. When it was his turn to compete, he turned in a record low score. People must have thought I was crazy, beaming with pride as I was.

On the way home, I bought Arnold his very own Big Mac and a milk shake—as I had promised I'd do if he kept his choppers off the other dogs at the match.

It was possible to live with Arnold after that. He was never perfect, but he had some remarkable qualities. I wouldn't want to go through the experience of training a crazy animal again, but I'm glad I did it once. He taught me a lot, that dog.

MONDO CANINE

THE DOGS

IN MY LIFE

IAN SHOALES

Where to begin? Like Nabokov, I'd like to command, "Speak Memory,

speak! Good Memory!" But the very first dog in my life figures mainly as a pre-memory: she was a bulldog named Princess who, my mother says, terrified me. I was three at the time; my father was in Korea. The proud owners of Princess were in the habit, according to my mother, of pushing her around the block in a baby carriage. Princess loved these strolls so much that whenever she was out on her own, and happened to see a baby carriage, she'd try to jump in. This behavior did not endear Princess to the mothers and babies of the neighborhood.

But let's return to my terror. My mother had a theory about it: seeing a dog, an *ugly* dog, where a baby ought to be just blew to flinders my tiny preconceptions of the way the world worked. The bulldog in the baby carriage triggered a pre-LSD experience, if you get what I'm saying, thrusting me into an Alice-in-Wonderland/ Franz Kafka reality. I had as much of a psychotic reaction, in short, as a moppet can muster, causing me to run away from the baby carriage, hysterical, screaming and inconsolable. It must have been a Major Problem Area in the child-psych department, judging by the number of times my mother has told this goddam story, usually to complete strangers.

But I don't remember any of this. I have only one memory of Princess, a memory which played a large role in the formation of my mature (so to speak) sexuality. But we'll get to that. For now, let's leave Princess, and say only that she seemed to embody most of the qualities '50s America looked for in a dog; that is, she was lovable yet mildly annoying, ugly in a cute sort of way, and famous in the neighborhood.

When my father returned from Korea, he brought with him a deck of cards featuring 52 different naked Korean women, a tube which revealed a naked Korean woman when held up to a light, and the only "war" story I ever heard him tell, about a Korean family, discovered by a squeamish squad of G.I.s, eating a dog. (These horrified rumors, by the way, that third-world folks eat dogs at the drop of a hat are among the more bizarre manifestations of racism. I've heard these tales about Vietnamese refugees—"It's true! They trap 'em right there in Golden Gate Park!"—, American Indians—"It's part of their peyote rituals or something"—, and Mexicans—"I wouldn't eat them tacos." Even if these stories *were* true, gosh, maybe these people were *hungry*. Hey, if I was living in a bomb crater, thousands of miles from a Kentucky Fried, I'd eat Rover too.)

When pressed, my father admitted he hadn't seen the dog-devouring himself. As a matter of fact, when I finally worked up the nerve in the mid-'60s to call my father a condescending neoimperialist for telling this story, it was the first of many occasions that he kicked me out of the house. On such occasions, I'd usually spend the night on my girlfriend's couch with Blackie, her sullen Labrador. Many times I'd wake up in the middle of the night to find Blackie's face inches from mine, motionless, staring at me. He'd be making this *noise*, halfway between a growl and a whimper. I didn't know if he wanted to lick my face or tear out my throat. Come to think of it, I had similar doubts about my girlfriend, who later threw me over for a Mormon with a drinking problem. But that's another story for another time.

The cruel truth is, *I never had a dog as a child.* My father had grown up on a farm, and the idea of keeping an animal as a *pet* struck him as foolish and decadent. "What do you want a dog for?" he'd say to me, "You aren't blind and we don't raise sheep."

Faced with this attitude I could only content myself with the glorious dogs of fiction: Jim Kjelgaard's *Big Red*, the seeing eye dog from *Follow My Leader* (the first work of pop culture in my experience to feature the exchange, "Go ahead, Doc, take the bandages off." "They—*are* off, Tommy."), Old Yeller, The Shaggy Dog and D.A., dogs of Flanders and Disney—true blue dogs who fetched ducks, pulled icy sleds over tundras, and lugged grenades and radios through the steaming jungles of the Pacific Theatre of Operations. All I wanted, when I grew up, was a manly squint and a deep voice with which to command my wonder dog: "Lassie, fetch Timmy," or "Bring me the lug wrench, Rinty," or "Bullet, take the jeep and get the doc. I think my leg's broke," or "King, this case is closed!"

My childhood swarmed with little Scotties whining by their masters' graves, brave little Benjies, tireless mutts trotting the long miles home, fierce beasts closing mighty jaws around the wrists of bad guys, forcing them to drop their revolvers: "Good dog, Lad! Now bring it to me!"

Reader's Digest! Boy's Life! Saturday Evening Post! From these pages dogs bounded in great leaps, to yelp for help as perfect homes filled with smoke. They lugged babies through howling storms, and *still* found time to fetch, roll over, wrestle, sleep beside you at the Old Fishin' Hole, and even pose patiently for comic photographs in *Life:* wearing sunbonnets or big silly sunglasses, sporting false teeth, sitting in baby carriages— Even today, the Heartwarming Dog shows up on slow-news-day soundbites: surfing dogs, Frisbee-snatching dogs, drug-sniffing dogs, dogs that guide the deaf, lifeguard dogs. We even have *Good Dog Carl* and William Wegman's Man Ray photographs for the *ironic* dog lover.

And there's the flip side of the dog-as-tool: the security dog, the snarling Doberman, the sly German shepherd, the rabid St. Bernard. This is the tool gone out of control, the pit bull's lock of a jaw at a bitter master's command. In the deep woods somewhere, the ecstatic wailing of hounds must still be heard, as they corner some wild creature. Men with loaded weapons still amble to the kill, making mean jokes as they pass the bottle back and forth.

These are the dogs of our hopes and fears. Dogs in the real world don't always survive their adventures. For example, there was Swinburne, a Great Dane, who roamed my hometown at will, leaping happily on small children, knocking them over, sending them home in tears. One day Swinburne's body, riddled with shotgun pellets, was discovered at the city dump. Who knows what Swinburne's crime against his assassin had been? Every small town has a subculture of gun lovers with a grudge against the pesky. His killer was never found, but his murder was a front page story in the local paper, proving Swinburne's legendary status in my hometown. Contrast this to New York City, where the dogs are leashed and pooper-scoopered, and the only bodies found in dumps are the remains of underbosses. And, of course, I am familiar with the stories of Manhattan poodles, driven insane by the constraints of condo-dwelling, who leap willfully to their deaths from the tiny patios of high-rises. I admit it. I believe these stories.

A dog is not an urban creature. A dog belongs on a porch, or sleeping in the middle of the dirt road of some sun-baked township. A dog belongs in the back of a pickup, or following two steps behind its hippie owner. A dog should carry a tennis ball or a stick in its mouth. If possible, it should have a red bandana wrapped around its neck.

For 27 days in the early '70s I lived on a communal farm. The five dogs that lived there had formed a pack, eating and/or frightening our neighbor's chickens. This behavior did not endear the dogs to our farming neighbors. My fellow communards, naturally, believed that dogs should run wild, run free. I went along with this, until a car drove by one day, and somebody inside pointed a rifle at us, then drove on. I promptly got in my VW and drove on too. They weren't my dogs, and I was damned if I was going to get shot for them—an attitude, by the way, which was a pretty close analog of my feelings towards the Viet Nam War.

Just two weeks before, on a stoned hippie whim, we'd packed all the dogs and two cats into my VW, because somebody had heard it was Free Distemper Shots Night at some progressive veterinary clinic in the state capital. So I drove the two hours to Capital City with the dogs, the cats, a folksinger, his twelve-string, and a lesbian heroin addict who was into macrobiotics. (Ah, those were the days!) When we arrived, the clinic was closed. The folksinger and lesbian decided to stay, and I had to drive back to the farm alone—well, not *alone*, with a whining, spitting mass of fur and muscle. It reminded me of a similar trip I'd made, back in 1968, in the same VW,

MONDO CANINE

with a retarded woman, a registered nurse, and two Norwegian elkhounds dying from a rare kidney disease. But that's a tale for which the world is not yet prepared.

The point is, up to a point, I was a sap for a dog. A dog was a tool for me no less than a hound for a hunter. The function of the dog, at that point in time, was to be an object of amusement while I was under the influence of illicit drugs. Dogs, you might say, occupied roughly the same place in my life that cable television does today. Of course I would never drive two hours to take my cable-ready television to a free clinic in the state capital. Especially not in a '65 VW. One does not have the same sentimental attachment.

But that point is moot. I don't have a cable-ready television, any more than I had a dog as a child. Now I realize how pathetic that sounds. When you talk about dogs, frankly, the pathetic is hard to avoid. But if you're starting to picture me as some little Ian-dog, wide-eyed, looking up at you at your feast, hoping for a scrap, a pat on the head, *attention* in short, well, it might not be the *hippest* of mental images, but I'll go with it. *I'll go all the way with it.*

When I was in 7th grade, on the bathetic brink of puberty, my mother in her frugal wisdom bought me a pair of pants from a mail-order catalogue. I was not popular, even though I possessed a certain inchoate intelligence, a gift for lip, and a genuine flair for self-destructive behavior—you know, throwing dirt lumps at the shiny souped-up cars of sociopathic juveniles, starting small fires on the edge of town, that sort of thing. Well, to make a long story short, on my way from Homeroom to History one morning, my mail-order pants split at the seams. They just fell apart. They looked, in their spontaneous disintegration, like a pair of chaps from a cowboy movie, only there were no weather-beaten chinos beneath them, just the pale flesh of my troubled legs. Mortified, I fled the school and ran home through the back alleys, weeping, cursing under my breath, hating my parents, God, the school system, President Kennedy's physical fitness program, my hometown, my state, shoddy workmanship in boys' clothing, the mail-order business in particular, capitalism in general, and— myself.

Yes, I, I, *I* bore the brunt of my rage and humiliation. My self-loathing was bottomless as I raced home, pants flapping like the tattered sails of a schooner racked by the winds of a ruthless sea. *Would I had never been born!* was my thoughts' gist, as tears squirted from my eyes, to fall behind me with a noise like bursting water balloons. My reasoning was this: if I'd never been *born*, I wouldn't *get* into fistfights every morning before Homeroom, my father's blood pressure would go down, my sister would no longer suffer dutch-rub agonies at my hands, my mother could use my bedroom for a sewing room, communists would discard their nuclear weapons, lions and lambs would lie down together, and the *Pants From Hell would never have been ordered in the first place!*

It was in the turbulent center of this matrix of misery that I rounded the corner of my block to see an ambulance parked in front of the Dorfmanns', two doors up from us. As I ran past, hoping to be such a blur of motion that, like the Flash, I would achieve invisibility, I noticed two men in white carrying Mr. Dorfmann down the front steps, his wife framed in the doorway above him, her mouth a quivering zero of concern. I learned later that he'd had a heart attack (he recovered), but such was the egotism of my self-pity that I believed my *very presence* in the vicinity, my alarming state of mind, had acted in some hideous psychokinetic manner hitherto unknown to science, and *killed* poor Mr. Dorfmann.

When I got home, all the doors were locked (cautious Mother was out shopping), so I went under the backyard lilac bush, hunkered down, and gave out great snorkeling sobs that put every bird within a five block radius to flight. They wheeled like vultures in the sky above me. My plan was to sit there, sniffling, until all my ducts dried up. I'd dehydrate, turn to dust, and blow away. *This was a good plan.*

But then Skipper came along.

Skipper was our next-door neighbors' dog, a black cocker spaniel who, at that point in time, was wearing a plaster cast that covered his lower torso, and held his right hind leg immobile at a slight angle away from his body. Skipper's hip had been broken a month before, by (the neighborhood assumed) an angry tennis player from the public court down the street. Skipper loved to chase balls, whether people were playing fetch with him or not. He had the habit of bounding enthusiastically into the middle of matches, and making spectacular leaps six or seven feet into the air to catch balls in mid-play. This behavior did not endear Skipper to lovers of tennis.

MONDO
CANINE

Immediately after his owners had brought Skipper home from the vet in his glowing white cast, Skipper disappeared for a week. We thought he'd met the same fate as Swinburne, but he showed up finally, cast filthy, coat matted, tail wagging, with a dirty gray tennis ball in his mouth, which he dropped at his master's feet. Then he barked twice, in what I can only assume were triumph and joy.

So Skipper came along, limping energetically, tail lolling, a tennis ball held hopefully in his mouth. I wrapped my arms around his neck and wailed, "I'm hugging my neighbor's dog. I don't have a dog, America! *I have to hug someone else's dog!*" Then Skipper dropped the ball at my feet and barked twice.

So I threw the damn ball for Skipper until my mother came home, and another emotional crisis passed, thanks to Man's Best Friend. Which brings me back to Princess.

One day, I was playing in front of our house. I couldn't have been much older than four. It was autumn. The leaves were changing colors and falling. The noon whistle had just blown. Four teenage girls were sitting in front of our house, out of sight of the nearby high school, in a gray boxy parked car, casually inhaling cigarettes before they had to go back to class. Because I was the child of parents who only got in a car to *go* somewhere, I was baffled by their just sitting there. So I walked up to the car, intending to ask them what the deal was.

At that moment Princess came waddling along, with what was probably a grin but at the time seemed like a foaming snarl on her mashed-in face. I lost my head. I started running for the gray car and girls like a swimmer trying to make the island before the sharks got him. As I started to scream, so did the girls, and the back door opened, and they hauled me in.

Screams turned to giggles as the back door slammed. I found myself sitting between two girls with plucked eyebrows and grown-up eyes. As I peered around the girl on my right, I could just see the top of Princess' ugly head as she stood on her hind legs to look in the window. She was whining with desire, probably thinking this was the biggest baby carriage she'd ever seen. The girl on my right stopped giggling, rolled down the window, and started to scratch Princess behind her ears. "She won't hurtcha," the girl said to me. "It's just old Princess. See? Everybody knows old Princess."

MONDO
CANINE

"I'm Ian," I volunteered. The front seat girls ignored me and returned to their furious smoking and whispered gossip. "I live right up there," I said proudly. I was trying to impress them, break the ice.

I looked at the girl on my left. She gave me a weary smile and frenched her Pall Mall, pulling up twin columns of smoke from her parted lips into her flared nostrils. I can't begin to tell you how glamorized I was by this. Then she blew the smoke out the window, and we all fell into a silence broken only by the damp panting of Princess.

"Where you going?" I asked.

The girl behind the wheel didn't even bother to turn around. "Crazy," she said, bored. "Want to come along?"

I began to nod my head furiously. "Yes," I said. "Yes, yes, yes!" I was bouncing up and down on the seat in what feminists would, years later, term a pre-orgasmic state.

But they didn't take me anywhere. My mother came and retrieved me. I can still see them recede behind me, four delinquent girls and an ugly dog, as my mother carried me into the house and a constantly alarming future. This is my earliest memory.

And so the puppies of innocence grow to be the wild dogs snarling in the back of the adult psyche. But I still remember the vicious beasts as they once were, sweet little guys abandoned on the front steps of my childhood id—the little fluffy one called Desire for Escape, the wiry nervous one called A Mother's Love, the yellow-eyed wolfling called The Brief Attention of Restless Teenage Girls.

No, there is no lack of hellhounds to dog a poor boy's heels, but it's always the *runt* of the litter, the little tail-wagger so ugly it's cute, wanting no more than love, that's the scary nameless one. It's always the harmless that prey on my mind. Maybe there's just no place for puppy love in a dog-eat-dog world. I dunno. I gotta go.

MONDO CANINE

I, DOG

I was born a yellow pup; date, locality, pedigree and weight unknown.
. . . I grew up to be an anonymous yellow cur looking like a cross
between an Angora cat and a box of lemons.

> ■ O. HENRY,
> *"MEMOIRS OF A YELLOW DOG"*

My father was a St. Bernard, my mother was a Collie, but I am a
Presbyterian. This is what my mother told me; I do not know these nice
distinctions myself.

> ■ MARK TWAIN,
> *"AILEEN MAVOURNEEN"*

I am his Highness' dog at Kew;
Pray tell me, sir, whose dog are you?

> ■ ALEXANDER POPE

My name is MacDunald, and I'm as braw a Scot as ever chewed up a
pair of slippers. I'm stubborn and I'm canny, I'm short-legged and close
to the ground; what I lack in size I make up in courage. The Scotch
are a fighting race and the tartan of my clan has never dragged the
dust, my breed has never known defeat and we die game, do we Scots.
My hair is coarse and wiry and my tail is carried high. I want to tell
you these facts so you won't think me a sissy even if I do live a soft life
in a fashionable neighborhood.

> ■ JOHN HELD,
> *"MacDUNALD"*

They tell me a cat can look at a king. Well, I have shaken paws with
two Presidents of the United States, one Vice-President, one former

213

Pete the Dog, canine star of the "Our Gang" comedies.

Secretary of State, more governors than I can wag my tail at, and the ambassador from Japan. My head has been rubbed by Jacqueline Onassis, Paul McCartney, Lady Bird Johnson, Beverly Sills, Sammy Davis, Gretchen Wyler and John V. Lindsay. Otto Preminger, Tony Randall, Leslie Uggams, Dick Van Dyke, Dinah Shore, Robert Wagner and Natalie Wood have fondled my ears, and I have been petted by Lauren Bacall, Barbra Streisand, Jack Albertson, Jean Stapleton and Anne Bancroft. Once I even growled and showed my teeth to Muhammad Ali, and the heavyweight champion of the world backed down. Andy Warhol took my picture, and so did Richard Avedon. That one was printed in *Vogue*. I made Ethel Merman and Bob Hope laugh. I have worn my black bow tie to a White House reception, at which I entertained President and Mrs. Carter and they entertained me. I've worn the same tie to the Tony Awards and to Sardi's restaurant, which is a favorite hangout for all us theater folk. I guess you'd call me a star.

■ SANDY (THE CANINE STAR OF *ANNIE*),
THE AUTOBIOGRAPHY OF A STAR

215

My name is Mildred Kerr Bush and I came to live with the Bush family on February 13, 1987. Their previous dog, C. Fred Bush, had died on January 20 and George, who was then Vice-President of the United States of America, knew that Bar missed him and needed a dog. . . . I'm going to be honest (this is a confession that is difficult for me to make and you will understand why as you read on). Bar did whisper to me that night, "You are *so* sweet, but you are *so* ugly. You have a pig's nose, you are bowlegged, and your eyes are yellow." I knew immediately that I was going to have to try harder. She also told me that she really loved me. I believed her.

■ MILLIE,
MILLIE'S BOOK

I'm a lean dog, a keen dog, a wild dog, and lone;
I'm a rough dog, a tough dog, hunting on my own;
I'm a bad dog, a mad dog, teasing silly sheep;
I love to sit and bay at the moon and keep fat souls from sleep.

I'll never be a lap dog, licking dirty feet,
A sleek dog, a meek dog, cringing for my meat,
Not for me the fireside, the well-filled plate,
But shut door, and sharp stone, and cuff and kick and hate.

Not for me the other dogs, running by my side,
Some have run a short while, but none of them would bide.
O mine is still the lone trail, the hard trail, the best,
Wide wind, and wild stars, and hunger of the quest!

> ■ IRENE RUTHERFORD McLEOD,
> *"LONE DOG"* from
> *SONGS TO SAVE A SOUL*

216

Every dog should have a man of his own. There is nothing like a well-behaved person around the house to spread the dog's blanket for him, or bring him his supper when he comes home man-tired at night.

> ■ COREY FORD,
> *"EVERY DOG SHOULD HAVE A MAN"*

Freckles, my boy, was a kind of Public Character, too. He went around bragging about my noble blood and bravery, and all the other boys and dogs in town sort of looked up to him and thought how lucky he was to belong to a dog like me. And he deserved whatever glory he got out of it, Freckles did. For, if I do say it myself, there's not a dog in town got a better boy than my boy Freckles, take him all in all. I'll back him against any dog's boy that is anywhere near his size, for

MONDO
CANINE

fighting, swimming, climbing, foot-racing, or throwing stones farthest and straightest. Or I'll back him against any stray boy, either.

■ DON MARQUIS,
"BEING A PUBLIC CHARACTER"

It's not too hard to train a human to open a door when you bark to go out, but it's often something else when it comes to using flea powder and clean kennel bedding. And while humans are generally pretty understanding about needing to play once in a while, why can't they get it through their thick heads that a dog, who doesn't wear shoes, finds it hard to tell an old one that ought to be chewed from a new one that shouldn't. It seems that people are basically inconsistent and confusing; they take an old brown chair that you liked to curl up in and cover it all yellow and won't let you come near it. Do they think that yellow is bad for a dog, or what?

■ GENE HILL,
"EVERY DOG SHOULD HAVE A MAN"

Sirius classified human beings in respect of their attitude to dogs; and even in later life he found this a useful touchstone of human character. There were those who were simply indifferent to dogs, lacking sufficient imagination to enter into any reciprocal relation with them. There were the "dog lovers," whom he detested. These were folks who sentimentalized dogs, and really had no accurate awareness of them, exaggerating their intelligence and loveableness, mollycoddling them and over-feeding them; and starving their natural impulses of sex, pugnacity and hunting. For this sort, dogs were merely animate and "pathetically human" dolls. Then there were the dog-detesters, who were either too highbrow to descend to companionship with a dumb animal or too frightened of their own animal nature. Finally there were the "dog-interested," who combined a fairly accurate sense of the difference between dog and man with a disposition to respect a dog *as a dog,* as a remote but essentially like-minded relative.

■ OLAF STAPLEDON,
SIRIUS

Whoo-oo-oo-hooh-hoo-oo! Oh, look at me, I am perishing in this gateway. The blizzard roars a prayer for the dying, and I howl with it. I am finished, finished. That bastard in the dirty cap—the cook of the Normal Diet Cafeteria for employees of the People's Central Economic Soviet—threw boiling water at me and scalded my left side. The scum, and he calls himself a proletarian! Lord, o lord, how it hurts! hurts! my side is cooked to the bone. And now I howl and howl, but what's the good of howling?

■ MIKHAIL BULGAKOV,
"HEART OF A DOG"

Now, I am a mixer. I can't help it. It's my nature. I like men. I like the taste of their shoes, the smell of their legs, the sound of their voices. It may be weak of me, but a man has only to speak to me, and a sort of thrill goes right down my spine and sets my tail wagging.

■ P. G. WODEHOUSE,
A VERY SHY GENTLEMAN

I have little in the way of material things to leave. Dogs are wiser than men. They do not waste their days hoarding property. They do not ruin their sleep worrying about how to keep the objects they have, and to obtain the objects they have not. There is nothing of value I have to bequeath except my love and my faith. . . . Dogs do not fear death as men do. We accept it as part of life, not as something terrible and alien which destroys life. . . . One last word of farewell, Dear Master and Mistress. Whenever you visit my grave, say to yourselves with regret but also with happiness in your hearts: "Here lies one who loved us and whom we loved." No matter how deep my sleep I shall hear you, and not all the power of death can keep my spirit from wagging its grateful tail.

■ EUGENE O'NEILL,
"THE LAST WILL AND TESTAMENT OF
SILVERDENE EMBLEM O'NEILL"

wauwinet, nantucket Island, mass.

dear aunt mimi and uncle philip,

Summertime again and dogs writing letters but i thought you'd like to know whether or not I was dead. early on wednesday morning he rolled me over unceremoniously to see if I was en rut and then we made a hurried start, one step ahead of the county trust co. and the collection agency for rabin's bootery inc. it was the usual guttapercha—don't put your head out the window cassie, don't bark at the lady cassie, be a gude dog, cassie, etcsteta. . . .

In the morning we took the steamer which was nothing for dogs. himself spent practically the whole voyage looking behind newspapers and under hat brims to see if there wasn't anybody he knew. then we came to this quaint old fashioned village where he tried to kite a check. the only reason he ever came to nantucket being that he figured they wouldn't hear his checks bounce this far out to sea. . . .

. . . I've come in for a lot of criticism because I rescue strange children and try to board strange boats but how they love to see me dive into a high surf and ride back on a comber with a piece of driftwood in my teeth and a silly grin on my face. how they squeal. give my love to mother. she is never far from my thoughts.

yr. XXX obedient chg.
Cassie

■ JOHN CHEEVER,
THE LETTERS OF JOHN CHEEVER

219

Long ago . . . we made a covenant with man. We were the first animal to make covenant and brought him the cows, sheep, horses: all the others. We hunted his meat, guarded his flocks, his home and his children. On our bellies we went into narrow dens after creatures with sharp teeth. We have hunted foxes and wolves and bears and lions because he wished it. At his behest we have killed our own kind. We will die for him. Free dogs made covenant with man: we made him master.

. . .

We made no food covenant. . . . We are not woolies that would die without shepherds to tend them. Free dogs hunt their own meat. We only asked that the master keep us in his wonderful eyes. But masters no longer keep us. They have forgotten the old time when they were alone and terrified on the darkening plain. They have forgotten their first ally against the night. Oh, they are so foolish! Like young puppies turned loose with stock, they rush here and there, exciting themselves for no reason but excitement itself. Like puppies, they are hurtful one moment, forgetful the next. They do not keep us in their eyes. They do not trouble to see us. ■ DONALD McCAIG, *NOP'S TRIALS*

THE DOG WHO

PAID CASH

WILL ROGERS

While I didn't have anything else to do, I got to watching an old spot-

ted dog. He was just an ordinary dog, but when I looked at him close, he was alert and friendly with everyone. Got to inquiring around and found out he'd been bumped off a freight train and seemed to have no owner. He made himself at home and started right in business. When a crowd of cowboys would go into a saloon, he would follow 'em in and begin entertaining. He could do all kinds of tricks—turn somersaults, lay down and roll over, sit up on his hind feet, and such like.

He would always rush to the door and shake hands with all the newcomers. The boys would lay a coin on his nose, and he'd toss it high in the air and catch it in his mouth and pretend to swallow it. But you can bet your life he didn't swallow it—he stuck it in one side of his lip, and when he got a lip full of money, he'd dash out the back door and disappear for a few minutes. What he had really done was hide his money. As soon as he worked one saloon, he would pull out and go to another place.

I got to thinking while watching this old dog, how much smarter he is than me. Here I am out of a job five hundred miles from home and setting around and can't find a thing to do, and this old dog hops off a train and starts right in making money, hand over fist.

Me and some boys around town tried to locate his hidden treasure, but this old dog was too slick for us. He never fooled away no time on three or four of us boys that was looking for work. He seemed to know we was broke, but he was very friendly. As he was passing along by me, he'd wag his tail and kinda wink. I musta looked hungry and forlorn. I think he wanted to buy me a meal.

When times was dull and he got hungry, he would mysteriously disappear. Pretty soon he'd show up at a butcher shop with a dime in his mouth and lay it on the counter and the butcher would give him a piece of steak or bone. He always paid for what he got in the line of grub. Pretty soon he seemed to get tired of the town, and one morning he was gone. A railroad man told us later that he seen the same dog in Trinidad, Colorado.

DOGS THAT HAVE KNOWN ME
BY JEAN KERR

It's not just our own dogs that bother me. The dogs I meet at parties are even worse. I don't know what I've got that attracts them; it just doesn't bear thought. My husband swears I rub chopped meat on my ankles. But at every party it's the same thing. I am sitting in happy conviviality with a group in front of the fire when all of a sudden the large mutt of mine host appears in the archway. Then, without a single bark of warning, he hurls himself upon me. It always makes me think of that line from *A Streetcar Named Desire*—"Baby, we've had this date right from the beginning." My martini flies into space and my stockings are torn before he finally settles down peacefully in the lap of my new black faille. I blow out such quantities of hair as I haven't swallowed and glance at my host, expecting to be rescued. He murmurs, "Isn't that wonderful? You know, Brucie is usually so distant with strangers."

At a dinner party in Long Island last week, after I had been mugged by a large sheep dog, I announced quite piteously, "Oh dear, he seems to have swallowed one of my earrings." The hostess looked really distressed for a moment, until she examined the remaining earring. Then she said, "Oh, I think it will be all right. It's small and it's round."

FIRST DOGS

Thirty-three out of forty-one U.S. presidents have owned dogs. George Washington kept a large number of hounds (Chaunter, Mopsy, Truelove, Vulcan) and Abraham Lincoln actually had a mutt named Fido. Teddy Roosevelt had a bullterrier named Pete, Woodrow Wilson an Airedale named Davie, and Warren G. Harding's Laddie Boy sat in on cabinet meetings and once gave an interview to the Washington *Star*.

Franklin D. Roosevelt's Scottie, Fala, slept in his master's bedroom and was the object of a vicious rumor during the 1944 presidential campaign. The Republicans charged that Roosevelt had abused his office by sending a U.S. Navy destroyer to retrieve Fala, allegedly left behind on a remote island during a tour of Alaska. Roosevelt's canny response to the charge turned the tables on the Republicans:

> Republican leaders have not been content with attacks on me, or my wife, or my sons. No, not content with that, they now include my little dog, Fala. Well, of course, *I* don't resent attacks and my *family* doesn't resent attacks, but Fala does resent them. You know, Fala

Reagan First Dog "Lucky"
performing one of his
last official acts.

Checkers Nixon, circa 1952.

is Scotch, and being a Scottie, as soon as he learned that the Republican fiction writers had concocted a story that I had left him behind on the Aleutian Islands and had sent a destroyer back to find him—at a cost to the taxpayers of two or three or eight or twenty million dollars—his Scotch soul was furious. He has not been the same dog since.

The Bettmann Archive

Fala and his master.

MONDO
CANINE

Lyndon B. Johnson had several First Dogs, including the beagles, Him (famous for having his ears unceremoniously pulled by the president; he was later run over and killed by a car while chasing a squirrel on the White House grounds) and Her, who died after swallowing a rock. A lesser-known Johnson First Dog was Blanco, a white collie who was put on tranquilizers after growling inhospitably at the visiting canine superstar, Lassie.

Richard Nixon's First Dogs included a Yorkshire terrier (Pasha), a miniature poodle (Vicky) and an Irish setter (King Timahoe). But the Nixons' most famous dog never made it to the White House, though he unwittingly helped deflect charges of financial misdealings during the 1952 presidential campaign and thereby helped save his master's political life. Amid revelations of a "slush fund" that Nixon had received from a group of California supporters, and in response to mounting pressure on Eisenhower to drop him as a running mate, Nixon went on national television to deny that any of the money went for his personal use. In a brilliant half-hour address now known as The Checkers Speech, Nixon painstakingly listed all his assets and liabilities, and in the interest of "full disclosure," he revealed that he had received—and *kept*—a gift from a political supporter:

> A man down in Texas heard Pat on the radio mention the fact that our two youngsters would like to have a dog. And, believe it or not, the day before we left on this campaign trip we got a message from Union Station in Baltimore saying they had a package for us. We went down to get it. You know what it was? It was a little cocker spaniel dog in a crate that he sent all the way from Texas. Black and white spotted. And our little girl Tricia, the six-year-old, named it Checkers. And you know, the kids love the dog, and I just want to say this right now, that regardless of what they say about it, *we're gonna keep it!*"

The speech was a huge success: Eisenhower kept Nixon on the ticket and they were elected to the first of two terms.

A TOUR OF THE BUSH WHITE HOUSE

MR. DONALDSON: You know, we can't avoid it any longer. Millie has joined us.

MRS. BUSH: Come here, Mill. Millie's always with me. She's my shadow.

MR. DONALDSON: Now, I've got to ask you something.

MRS. BUSH: Yes?

MR. DONALDSON: How did you react when *The Washingtonian* magazine said she was the ugliest dog around?

MRS. BUSH: Millie is pretty ugly right now.

MR. DONALDSON: Millie, stop that. We're on national television, Millie!

President Lyndon B. Johnson used to lift his dog by the ears—
the dog's ears. Eventually he tore the ears off, but that didn't
matter much: the dog never came when he called.

VICTOR BORGE

The Reagans had two First Dogs, the hapless Lucky (who was eventually exiled to the Reagans' Santa Barbara ranch) and the cur-like Rex, often seen dragging Mrs. Reagan across the White House lawn.

But the all-time, paws-down publicity champ is Barbara Bush's spaniel, Millie, whose maternal and literary achievements, whose breezy, unaffected style, have distinguished her as the greatest First Dog in history.

THE DEATH
OF A DOG

The old dog [Cassie] is dead. . . . She lost the use of her legs on Sunday and her wits on Monday and I had the vet kill her yesterday afternoon. She was a wonderful companion and I loved her dearly but I shed very few tears. . . . We had her for fifteen years and she led a very active and useful life but when I last took her for a walk she fell in the deep snow and had to be carried home. Some years ago I went to a psychiatrist who told me I was obsessed with my Mother. When I told him that I like to swim he said: Mother. When I told him that I liked the rain he said: Mother. When I told him that I drank too much he said: Mother. This was all rubbish but sitting here with Cassie one evening I saw her raise her head exactly as Mother used to and give me a pained, sweet, fleeting smile that was unnerving.

■ JOHN CHEEVER,
THE LETTERS OF JOHN CHEEVER

Dear Mr. Norton,

When Teddy & I heard . . . of Taffy's sad taking-off we both really felt a personal regret in addition to our profound sympathy for his master.

His artless but engaging ways, his candid enjoyment of his dinner, his judicious habit of exercising by means of those daily rushes up & down the road, had for so many years interested & attracted us that he occupies a very special place in our crowded dog-memories. . . .

Somebody says "L'espoir est le plus fidèle des amants" [Hope is the

MONDO
CANINE

most faithful of lovers]—but I really think it should be put in the plural & applied to dogs. Staunch and faithful little lovers that they are, they give back a hundred fold every sign of love one ever gives them—& it mitigates the pang of losing them to know how very happy a little affection has made them.

■ EDITH WHARTON,
LETTER OF CONDOLENCE TO CHARLES ELIOT NORTON

It is strange how we buy our sorrow
For the touch of perishing things, idly, with open eyes:
How we give our hearts to brutes that will die in a few seasons.

■ J.C. SQUIRE,
A DOG'S DEATH

It was the saddest damn thing I ever saw, that small pretty woman all alone out there with nobody to help her, burying her dog.

I would have been glad to lend a hand, of course, once I realized what she was doing. But I had a feeling she needed to do it herself.

She had a real struggle getting him out to the yard. Basset hounds are squat but heavy. He was stretched out on his side, stiff-legged already, on a fuzzy pink bath mat, the kind that's supposed to look like fur—if you can imagine pink fur. She slid him down three steps from the back door. The way the carcass bumped down those steps made me grit my teeth. She was crazy about that dog. She dragged the mat across the grass toward the far corner of the house. Her eyes were closed.

. . . The clock on the stove said a quarter to eight. I put the coffee on to perk. Then, very quietly, I went out the front door and circled around the north side to the back. From behind a bank of gone-by lilacs, I could see her. She'd already started digging.

■ SUSAN DODD,
"HELL-BENT MEN AND THEIR CITIES"

Death, to a dog, is the final unavoidable compulsion, the last ineluctable scent on a fearsome trail, but they like to face it alone, going out into the woods, among the leaves, if there are any leaves when their time comes, enduring without sentimental human distraction the Last Loneliness, which they are wise enough to know cannot be shared by anyone. If your dog has to go, he has to go, and it is better to let him go alone.

■ JAMES THURBER,
"AND SO TO MEDVE"

234

Late one afternoon he wandered home, too slowly and uncertainly to be the Rex that had trotted briskly homeward up our avenue for ten years. I think we all knew when he came through the gate that he was dying. He had apparently taken a terrible beating, probably from the owner of some dog he had got into a fight with. His head and body were scarred, and some of the brass studs of his heavy collar were sprung loose. He licked at our hands and, staggering, fell, but got up again. We could see that he was looking for someone. One of his three masters was not home. He did not get home for an hour. During that hour the bull terrier fought against death as he had fought against the cold, strong current of the creek. When the person he was waiting for did come through the gate, whistling, ceasing to whistle, Rex walked a few wobbly paces toward him, touched his hand with his muzzle, and fell down again. This time he didn't get up.

■ JAMES THURBER,
"SNAPSHOT OF A DOG"

Now thou art dead, no eye shall ever see,
For shape and service, Spaniell like to thee.
This shall my love doe, give thy sad death one
Teare, that deserves of me a million.

■ ROBERT HERRICK,
HESPERIDES

Why, I tried to kill that Spot once—he was no good for anything—and I fell down on it. I led him out into the brush, and he came along slow and unwilling. He knew what was going on. I stopped in a likely place, put my foot on the rope, and pulled my big Colt's. And that dog sat down and looked at me. I tell you he didn't plead. He just looked. . . . And I want to tell you right now that it got beyond me. It was like killing a man, a conscious, brave man who looked calmly into your gun as much as to say, "Who's afraid?" . . . I got scared. I was trembly all over, and my stomach generated a nervous palpitation that made me seasick. I just sat down and looked at that dog, and he looked at me, till I thought I was going crazy. Do you want to know what I did? I threw down the gun and ran back to camp with the fear of God in my heart. ■ JACK LONDON,
"THAT SPOT"

No dog likes to die in the presence of human beings or under anybody's bed. It is a profound instinct in that species which makes it want to die alone and not with all its relatives around the bed. An old brown poodle up here crept away and hid in autumn leaves almost identically his own color, but he was found and dragged back home. This is a true and terrible story. It is probable that a dog would kill itself to avoid the kind of death it abhors. ■ JAMES THURBER,
SELECTED LETTERS

Muggs died quite suddenly one night. Mother wanted to bury him in the family lot under a marble stone with some such inscription as "Flights of angels sing thee to thy rest," but we pursuaded her it was against the law. In the end we just put up a smooth board above his grave along a lonely road. On the board I wrote with an indelible pencil "Cave Canem." Mother was quite pleased with the simple classic dignity of the old Latin epitaph. ■ JAMES THURBER,
"THE DOG THAT BIT PEOPLE"

MONDO CANINE

[Charles Dickens'] departure for America later that year involved good-byes at all his residences. Perhaps the most dramatic good-bye had already taken place in 1866. Now huge in size, Sultan . . . was docile and loving, though aggressively possessive. He had become his master's favorite, partly because of his affectionateness, partly because he rejected and detested everyone else. "So accursedly fierce towards other dogs" that he had to be muzzled in order to be taken out, he attacked everything moving or still, with a special "invincible repugnance to soldiers." Dashing "into the heart of a company . . . he pulled down an objectionable private." The price of such total love was the problem of how to deal with his creature's unmitigated enmity toward the rest of the world. To Dickens, he was the finest dog he had ever seen. "Between him and me there was a perfect understanding." Breaking his muzzle frequently, though, he came home "covered with blood again and again." One day he swallowed an entire blue-eyed kitten, afterward suffering "agonies of remorse (or indigestion)?" When he seized the little sister of one of the servants, Dickens flogged him. The next morning he took the dog to the meadow behind the house, accompanined by a half-dozen men with guns and a wheelbarrow. Sultan bounded out cheerfully, anticipating "the death of somebody unknown." He paused, meditatively, with his eyes on the wheelbarrow and the guns. "A stone deftly thrown across him . . . caused him to look round for an instant, and then he fell dead, shot through the heart."

■ FRED KAPLAN,
DICKENS, A BIOGRAPHY

MONDO
CANINE

AHBHU

HARLAN ELLISON

 Yesterday my dog died. For eleven years Ahbhu was my closest friend.

He was responsible for my writing a story about a boy and his dog that many people have read. He was not a pet, he was a person. It was impossible to anthropomorphize him, he wouldn't stand for it. But he was so much his own kind of creature, he had such a strongly formed personality, he was so determined to share his life with only those *he* chose, that it was also impossible to think of him as simply a dog. Apart from those canine characteristics into which he was locked by his species, he comported himself like one of a kind.

We met when I came to him at the West Los Angeles Animal Shelter. I'd wanted a dog because I was lonely and I'd remembered when I was a little boy how my dog had been a friend when I had no other friends. One summer I went away to camp and when I returned I found a rotten old neighbor lady from up the street had had my dog picked up and gassed while my father was at work. I crept into the woman's backyard that night and found a rug hanging on the clothesline. The rug beater was hanging from a post. I stole it and buried it.

At the Animal Shelter there was a man in line ahead of me. He had brought in a puppy only a week or so old. A Puli, a Hungarian sheep dog; it was a sad-looking little thing. He had too many in the litter and had brought this one to either be taken by someone else or to be put to sleep. They took the dog inside and the man behind the counter called my turn. I told him I wanted a dog and he took me back inside to walk down the line of cages.

In one of the cages the little Puli that had just been brought in was being assaulted by three larger dogs that had been earlier tenants. He was a little thing, and he was on the bottom, getting the stuffing knocked out of him. But he was struggling mightily.

"Get him out of there!" I yelled. "I'll take him, I'll take him, get him out of there!"

He cost two dollars. It was the best two bucks I ever spent.

Driving home with him, he was lying on the other side of the front seat staring at me. I had had a vague idea what I'd name a pet, but as I stared at him, and he stared back at me, I suddenly was put in mind of the scene in Alexander Korda's 1939 film *The Thief of Baghdad*, where the evil vizier, played by Conrad Veidt, had changed Ahbhu, the little thief, played by Sabu, into a dog. The film had superimposed the human over the canine face for a moment so there was an extraordinary look of intelligence in the face of the dog. The little Puli was looking at me with that same expression. "Ahbhu," I said.

He didn't react to the name, but then he couldn't have cared less. But that was his name, from that time on.

No one who ever came into my house was unaffected by him. When he sensed someone with good vibrations, he was right there, lying at their feet. He loved to be scratched, and despite years of admonitions he refused to stop begging for scraps at table, because he had found most of the people who came to dinner at my house were patsies unable to escape his woebegone Jackie-Coogan-as-the-Kid look.

But he was a certain barometer of bums, as well. On any number of occasions when I found someone I liked and Ahbhu would have nothing to do with him or her, it always turned out the person was a wrongo. I took to noting his attitude toward newcomers, and I must admit it influenced my own reactions. I was always wary of someone Ahbhu shunned.

Women with whom I had had unsatisfactory affairs would nonetheless return to the

MONDO
CANINE

house from time to time—to visit the dog. He had an intimate circle of friends, many of whom had nothing to do with me, and numbering among their company some of the most beautiful actresses in Hollywood. One exquisite lady used to send her driver to pick him up for Sunday afternoon romps at the beach.

I never asked him what happened on those occasions. He didn't talk.

Last year he started going downhill, though I didn't realize it because he maintained the manner of a puppy almost to the end. But he began sleeping too much, and he couldn't hold down his food—not even the Hungarian meals prepared for him by the Magyars who lived up the street. And it became apparent to me something was wrong with him when he got scared during the big Los Angeles earthquake last year. Ahbhu wasn't afraid of anything. He attacked the Pacific Ocean and walked tall around vicious cats. But the quake terrified him and he jumped up in my bed and threw his forelegs around my neck. I was very nearly the only victim of the earthquake to die from animal strangulation.

He was in and out of the veterinarian's shop all through the early part of this year, and the idiot always said it was his diet.

Then one Sunday when he was out in the backyard, I found him lying at the foot of the stairs, covered with mud, vomiting so heavily all he could bring up was bile. He was matted with his own refuse, and he was trying desperately to dig his nose into the earth for coolness. He was barely breathing. I took him to a different vet.

At first they thought it was just old age . . . that they could pull him through. But finally they took X rays and saw the cancer had taken hold in his stomach and liver.

I put off the day as much as I could. Somehow I just couldn't conceive of a world that didn't have him in it. But yesterday I went to the vet's office and signed the euthanasia papers.

"I'd like to spend a little time with him before," I said.

They brought him in and put him on the stainless steel examination table. He had grown so thin. He'd always had a pot-belly and it was gone. The muscles in his hind legs were weak, flaccid. He came to me and put his head into the hollow of my armpit. He was trembling violently. I lifted his head and he looked at me with the comic face I'd always thought made him look like Lawrence Talbot, the Wolf Man. He knew.

Sharp as hell right up to the end, hey old friend? He knew, and he was scared. He trembled all the way down to his spiderweb legs. This bouncing ball of hair that, when lying on a dark carpet, could be taken for a sheepskin rug, with no way to tell at which end head and which end tail. So thin. Shaking, knowing what was going to happen to him. But still a puppy.

I cried and my eyes closed as my nose swelled with the crying, and he buried his head in my arms because we hadn't done much crying at one another. I was ashamed of myself not to be taking it as well as he was.

"I *got* to, pup, because you're in pain and you can't eat. I *got* to." But he didn't want to know that.

The vet came in then. He was a nice guy, and he asked me if I wanted to go away and just let it be done.

Then Ahbhu came up out of there and *looked* at me.

There is a scene in Kazan's *Viva Zapata* where a close friend of Zapata's, Brando's, has been condemned for conspiring with the *federales*. A friend that had been with Zapata since the mountains, since the *revolución* had begun. And they come to the hut to take him to the firing squad, and Brando starts out, and his friend stops him with a hand on his arm, and he says to him with great friendship, "Emiliano, do it yourself."

Ahbhu looked at me and I know he was just a dog, but if he could have spoken with human tongue he could not have said more eloquently than he did with a look, *don't leave me with strangers.*

So I held him as they laid him down and the vet slipped the lanyard up around his right foreleg and drew it tight to bulge the vein, and I held his head and he turned it away from me as the needle went in. It was impossible to tell the moment he passed over from life to death. He simply laid his head on my hand, his eyes fluttered shut and he was gone.

I wrapped him in a sheet with the help of the vet and I drove home with Ahbhu on the seat beside me, just the way we had come home eleven years before. I took him out in the backyard and began digging his grave. I dug for hours, crying and mumbling to myself, talking to him in the sheet. It was a very neat, rectangular grave with smooth sides and all the loose dirt scooped out by hand.

I laid him down in the hole and he was so tiny in there for a dog who had seemed to be so big in life, so furry, so funny. And I covered him over and when the hole was packed full of dirt I replaced the neat divot of grass I'd scalped off at the start. And that was all.

But I couldn't send him to strangers.

THE END

THE MOST BEAUTIFUL GIRL IN THE WORLD

STANLEY BING

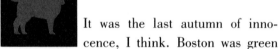

It was the last autumn of innocence, I think. Boston was green and gold and all kinds of bright orange, vermilion, and paisley, the air so crisp and fresh, and all things were possible. The Sox had just won the sixth game of the best World Series ever. Nixon had been gone for a year; drugs were still as American as scrapple; sex was safer than it would ever be again, at least physically. I was standing on the platform of the Red Line with my soon-to-be-ex-fiancée, Doris, who was bothering me about something, as she did between 1972 and 1976. It was early evening. Down at the end of the station sat a midsize ersatz collie dog, just beyond puppyhood, laughing. Her eyes glowed with a tremendous good nature and trust unencumbered by a surfeit of complicated insights. She was alone.

"Hi," I said. She came over, licked my hand discreetly, allowed herself to be scratched for a time, chased her tail in a dignified circle, lay down again. I remember thinking: "There are times God puts a choice in front of you." I often had such thoughts back then.

We took the dog.

She went totally nuts when she understood the news, bounding and leaping in a vertical parabola to kiss my face, and generally expressing an exuberance that made me want to laugh. As a world view, it was so inappropriate. Searching for the makings of a proto-leash, Doris found in her bottomless denim bag a hank of purple yarn, possibly the one she used for the three-year Sweater for Stan Project, the completion of which turned out to signify the end of our relationship. I wrapped several lengths around her neck—the dog's, that is—but it did not serve. To get her home in one piece, I had to pick her up and hold her like a baby. It is a silly position for a dog, and most fight it. Not her. She lay in my arms, feet poking skyward, head lolling back in a friendly grin, tongue draping out the corner of her mouth, eyes calmly investigating mine as if to say, "Hey, this is a nice idea. Why didn't you think of it before?"

At the time, I made $8,000 a year. My car was a pre-Nissan Datsun, basically a floorboard with wheels and perforated tin skin. My diet consisted of doughnuts, peanut butter, and Chef Boyardee ravioli straight from the can. Cold. My rent was $155 a month for six rooms. The sink was piled to eye level with every dish in the house, since Doris and I also couldn't get together on the politics of kitchen work.

I named the dog Elizabeth. Height: about thirty inches. Weight: thirty-five pounds. Eyes: brown. Tongue: red. Tail: rich and plumy. A coat of pure china white, so thick and lustrous and profuse that people would later suggest that I shear her and turn the output into a serape. In the summer she shed badly. In the winter, worse. All my clothes and furniture were coated with a fine layer of white flax. When she was young, her tummy was as pink as a baby's bottom, and she had a marvelous doggy smell, clean, pungent, yet sweet. Her personality? All I can say is that when the Lord made her, he forgot to add any malice, guile, or aggressiveness. Didn't chase squirrels, even. If another dog attacked her, she would roll over on her back immediately and expose her soft underbelly, clearly conveying the message: "Go ahead and kill me. I don't mind, but I think it would be a totally unnecessary waste of energy. But hey, just my opinion." Not once in her life was she hurt by any living creature.

Elizabeth was not smart, but she made the most of it. "She's the sweetest dog in the world," said a friend about her. "But she's got an IQ somewhere between a brick and a houseplant." When people asked what breed she was, we'd say, "Mexican

Brainless." How we'd laugh! In retrospect, this seems kind of unfair. Could she defend her thoughts, assuming she had any? Not at all. For all intents and purposes, she was mute: Not a bark, yelp, or whimper escaped her. In fourteen years, I heard her voice maybe three times. It was always a shock.

I broke up with Doris and rented a place that was nice before I got to it. I was not a master of business administration then, and it was not the living space of a responsible person. Many was the night Liz and I stayed up until dawn, eating biscuits and watching Charlie Chan. Her nose was big and black and wet and perfect for squeezing, and she liked nothing better than to sit at my side and lick my hand for hours on end. I think she got into a kind of trance when she did it, and I had to slap her around now and then to get her to stop.

No roommate could have suited me better. One afternoon, looking under my bed for a shoe to munch, she found a blue sphere covered with a gossamer pelt of fuzz. It had been an orange once, but now it was soft and alien to the touch. Any sensible person would have tossed it out immediately. I found her playing with it. Took a hell of a chase to get it away from her too.

Not long after, when the nation was spritzing its bicentennial all over itself, I met my soon-to-be future wife. Before long we were sort of living together. Dogs were not welcome in her building, so Elizabeth was forced to hold down the fort at my apartment. After a while, it became a dog's apartment, which I guess was only fair. Empty cans of her Alpo and my ravioli littered the rooms, and long skeins of toilet paper hung everywhere, for when Liz got bored, she loved to play with it, string it out, flip it over and under things. She tore into Hefty bags and distributed the contents. She kept herself occupied.

She also periodically ran away. If you opened a door or window, she was out it. One morning she tore through a screen and hurled herself to the street. I didn't blame her. The place was a pit. It was a good thing I lived on the ground floor.

She loved to run, that was it. I would take her to a nearby football field once every couple of days. It was fenced in. I'd let her off the leash, and she would sprint in an immense circle around the huge enclosure until I thought her heart would pop from exertion and joy. Then I'd pile her in the back of the car, where she'd sleep, heaving

MONDO CANINE

up and down as she dreamt, and shed. That was fine with me. It was a dog's car, too.

We got married, my wife and I, and for a while there Elizabeth was our only child. She got a lot of love. After a year, we moved to the city, and she, like us, learned to adjust to the demands of urban living. When we'd return home from a walk, I'd let her off the leash in the long hallway down to our three-room flat, and she'd tear down that corridor like a hound possessed, her tail tucked underneath her rear end for maximum aerodynamic lift and thrust, slam into the wall at the end, turn, and head back at even greater speed.

She was youth, and spirit, and dumb, careless vitality.

We were city people now, with city rituals. When we went to the mandatory summer community to visit friends, she was there, zipping freely down the beach in those days before the invention of deer ticks, chasing the waves until they crashed over her and I had to rescue her from the undertow. One night, we went back to eat sesame noodles and chicken, and our hostess put the salad on the floor since the table was full unto groaning. In the candlelight, as we talked, we heard a moist chomping sound, and a great smacking of lips. We looked underneath the table, and it was Liz, downing the last of the arugula and goat cheese and sun-dried tomatoes. She looked up at us, the vinaigrette glistening off her whiskers, as if to say, "Gosh, this is delicious, guys, but not that filling. How about some chicken bones to wash it down?"

To her, carcass of used poultry was the ultimate delicacy. One time, I left an entire oven-stuffer roaster wrapped in tinfoil on the kitchen counter. Two hours later, the only thing left in the room was a small piece of tinfoil and a grease spot on the floor. She had eaten not only the meat and bones, but the aluminum as well. I watched her for days, certain she had finally OD'd on her own sheer witlessness. But she hadn't.

She was indestructible.

She took the birth of our two kids with grace, even when they pulled her eyebrows or fell on her screaming and hugging and kissing her with the kind of passion adults usually reserve for the game-show hosts who award them cruises to Bimini. When my son was a year old, and particularly aggressive, he tried to ride her. She was thirteen by then, and growled at him. After some thought, it was determined that it was she who would be sent away to stay at my mother's house. The exile lasted six weeks. She went with the program after that.

One morning in 1988, she couldn't get up. I took her to the vet, who told me that her spleen was enlarged. Would I care to make a decision? After all, the dog was fourteen. We fixed her up. It was the best money I ever spent, and I spent a lot of it. While she was convalescing at the hospital, my son put together his first complete sentence: "I miss Wizbet," he said. And then he cried. How much is a dog's life worth?

Last winter we moved to a house with a backyard, a swing, and a piece of an acre. Elizabeth came, too.

So a month ago my wife and children went down to see my in-laws in Arizona. And the following Thursday, after breakfast, Liz fell down in the garden and just lay there, her eyes rolled up into her skull, heaving and panting and trembling. The episode lasted just a few minutes, but it scared me shitless. When she awoke, she was jolly and hungry, and spent the rest of the day in the backyard, staring off into space, always one of her favorite pastimes.

When she was falling down five times a day, the vet said to me, "You have to decide whether she is able to preserve her dignity leading this type of existence." I'd never considered it in those terms before. As she lay on her side, clearly not in the world as we know it, I held her paw and kissed her forehead, and all the fourteen years of my life with her swam before me and I knew, yes I did. And it was not a good knowing. I made a call. I put her in the car. My brother came along. We were both crying.

The vet's office was clean and cool. He's a nice guy, my vet. I got the feeling that he'd never get used to that part of his job. "This shot will put her to sleep easily," he said. "Then the next shot will put her to rest." He gave her the first and suddenly she arched her back and from her throat came a horrible, gut-wrenching cry, a raking, moaning howl that conveyed an understanding nobody needs to have, and for which none of us is ever ready. And my brother and I held her, and we were sobbing, and the vet said, "She's not in pain, she's just had a neurological reaction to the sedative." Then a few minutes later: "She's at peace." He was weeping, too.

MONDO CANINE

Her body was there, the coat still shiny, the nose still wet and warm. But *she* was gone. I noticed a small pulse in the tip of her tongue, which was hanging out of her mouth much as it had the very first night I saw her, in October of 1975, when Pete Rose was a hero and Boston was nine innings away from its first world championship in nearly six decades.

This is the last I will speak of her. I owe her this eulogy, dog to dog, for fourteen years of companionship, of laughs and devotion and cheek-by-jowl existence on this hard and incomprehensible planet.

THE SOUL

OF A DOG

DANIEL PINKWATER

 Once, Jill had fun with our Alaskan malamute, Arnold, by pretending that she was teaching him a nursery song. It was pure nonsense—Jill was tending our old-fashioned, nonautomatic clothes washer, and Arnold was keeping her company.

Jill sang him the song about the eensy beensy spider, and indicated where he was supposed to join in. He did so, with something between a scream of anguish and the call of a moose in rut.

The next time she had laundry to do, Arnold appeared, and sat squirming excitedly until she sang him the song. He came in on cue. Arnold learned a number of songs. His vocal range was limited, but his ear was good.

It was also Arnold who taught Juno, our other dog, to set up a howl whenever we passed a McDonald's. On a vacation trip, we'd breakfasted on Egg McMuffins for a week, and the dogs always got an English muffin. They never forgot.

I once observed Arnold taking care of an eight-week-old kitten. The kitten was in a cage. Arnold wanted to go and sleep in his private corner, but every time the kitten cried, he'd drag himself to his feet, slouch over to the cage and lie down with his nose between the wires, so the kitten could sink its tiny claws into it. When the kitten became quiet, Arnold would head for his corner and flop, exhausted. Immediately the kitten would cry, and Arnold would haul himself back to the cage. I counted this performance repeated over forty times.

Arnold acquired friends. People would visit him.

My friend Don Yee would borrow Arnold sometimes, and they'd drive to the White Castle and eat hamburgers.

He was the sort of dog you could talk things over with.

But he was not just a good listener, affable eccentric and bon vivant. He was a magnificent athlete. While Juno was tireless and efficient on the trail, Arnold made locomotion an art—a ballet.

Watching Arnold run flat-out in a large open space was unforgettable, and opened a window to something exceedingly ancient and precious—a link to the first time men followed dogs, and hunted to live.

He was a splendid companion—and he would pull you up a steep hill, if you were tired.

In a way, the hardest thing about living with dogs in modern times is related to the excellent care we give them.

Vast sums are spent by pet food companies devising beautifully balanced, cheap, palatable diets. Vet care these days is superb—and most pet owners take advantage of it.

As a result, dogs live longer than they may have done, and survive illnesses that they would not have survived in earlier times. And it very often falls to us to decide when a dog's life has to end—when suffering has come to outweigh satisfaction.

When it came Arnold's time to die, it was I who decided it. I called the vet and told him I was bringing Arnold in.

He knew about malamute vigor. He prepared a syringe with twice the dose it would take to put a dog Arnold's size to sleep. "Put to sleep" is an apt euphemism. It's simply an overdose of a sleeping drug. The dog feels nothing.

"There's enough in here for a gorilla," the vet wisecracked weakly. He was un-comfortable with what he had to do.

Arnold, of course, was completely comfortable—doing his best to put everyone else at ease.

I held Arnold while the vet tied off a vein.

"This will take six, maybe eight seconds at most," the vet said. He injected the fluid.

Nothing happened. Arnold, who had been completely relaxed, was now somewhat intent—but not unconscious, not dead.

"Sometimes it takes a little longer," the vet said. It had been a full half minute. Arnold was looking around.

The vet was perspiring—getting panicky. I knew what he was thinking. Some ghastly error. The wrong stuff in the syringe. More than a minute had passed.

A crazy thought occurred to me. Was it possible? Was Arnold waiting for me to give him leave to go? I rubbed his shoulders and spoke to him. "It's OK, Arnold, I release you." Instantly he died.

I swear I felt his spirit leave his body.

The vet and I went outside and cried for a quarter of an hour.

He was an awfully good dog.

OBITUARY

E. B. WHITE

Daisy ("Black Watch Debatable") died December 22, 1931, when she was hit by a Yellow Cab in University Place. At the moment of her death she was smelling the front of a florist's shop. It was a wet day, and the cab skidded up over the curb—just the sort of excitement that would have amused her, had she been at a safer distance. She is survived by her mother, Jeanine; a brother, Abner; her father, whom she never knew; and two sisters, whom she never liked. She was three years old.

Daisy was born at 65 West Eleventh Street in a clothes closet at two o'clock of a December morning in 1928. She came, as did her sisters and brothers, as an unqualified surprise to her mother, who had for several days previously looked with a low-grade suspicion on the box of bedding that had been set out for the delivery, and who had gone into the clothes closet because she had felt funny and wanted a dark, awkward place to feel funny in. Daisy was the smallest of the litter of seven, and the oddest.

Her life was full of incident but not of accomplishment. Persons who knew her only slightly regarded her as an opinionated little bitch, and said so; but she had a small circle of friends who saw through her, cost what it did. At Speyer Hospital, where she used to go when she was indisposed, she was known as "Whitey," because, the man told me, she was black. All her life she was subject to moods, and her feeling about horses laid her sanity open to question. Once she slipped her leash and chased a horse for three blocks through heavy traffic, in the carking belief that she was an effective agent against horses. Drivers of teams, seeing her only in the moments of her delirium, invariably leaned far out of their seat and gave tongue, mocking her; and thus made themselves even more ridiculous, for the moment, than Daisy.

She had a stoical nature and spent the latter part of her life an invalid, owing to an injury to her right hind leg. Like many invalids, she developed a rather objectionable cheerfulness, as though to deny that she had cause for rancor. She also developed, without instruction or encouragement, a curious habit of holding people firmly by the ankle without biting them—a habit that gave her an immense personal advantage and won her many enemies. As far as I know, she never even broke the thread of a sock, so delicate was her grasp (like a retriever's), but her point of view was questionable, and her attitude was beyond explaining to the person whose ankle was at stake. For my own amusement, I often tried to diagnose this quirkish temper, and I think I understand it: she suffered from a chronic perplexity, and it relieved her to take hold of something.

She was arrested once, by Patrolman Porko. She enjoyed practically everything in life except motoring, an exigency to which she submitted silently, without joy, and without nausea. She never took pains to discover, conclusively, the things that might have diminished her curiosity and spoiled her taste. She died sniffing life, and enjoying it.

TOP TEN WAYS
LIFE WOULD BE DIFFERENT
IF DOGS RAN THE WORLD

10. More Donahue shows about shedding.
9. Presidential candidates more likely to stop mid-speech and sniff base of podium.
8. Cats must report address to post office every year.
7. Procter & Gamble introduces new liver-flavored Crest.
6. Drinking from toilet no longer a faux pas.
5. Museums filled with still lifes of table scraps.
4. Constitutional amendment extends vote to wolves.
3. TV commercial altered so dog catches and devours little chuck wagon.
2. Monument in Washington commemorates "Our Neutered Brothers."
1. All motorists must drive with head out of car window.

■ DAVID LETTERMAN ON
"LATE NIGHT WITH DAVID LETTERMAN"

MOTORING!

To a country vet like myself whose life was spent on the roads and lanes these dogs were very important. The pattern was always the same, Dan stretched on the passenger seat with his head on my knee, Hector peering through the windshield, his paws balanced on my hand as it rested on the gear lever. Dan wasn't worried about what went on outside but Hector hated to miss a thing. His head bobbed around erratically as I changed gears but his feet never slipped off my hand.

■ JAMES HERRIOT,
JAMES HERRIOT'S DOG STORIES

My Scottie refused to go for a walk with a friend of the house, but she would joyously accompany any stranger who drove a car. On one occasion, after she had become totally blind, she escaped from the house and climbed into an immense van which was removing our furniture to another part of town. She established herself on the driver's seat, and sat there awaiting the departure with an air of ineffable satisfaction. She always delighted in motoring and this delight increased with her blindness. She had been a great hunter and, in my opinion, she re-captured something of the exhilaration of the chase in the swift movement of motoring. The car could not go too fast to please her. If it slowed down she would utter whines of protest. If it actually stopped, the whines would almost become howls. She never sat down in a car but stood, braced tense, facing the wind. Now and again she would turn her face toward me with an apologetic expression as though to say: "I have not fogotten that you are here but there are certain pleasures I cannot share with you." Her nose never ceased its sensitive quivering.

■ MAZO DE LA ROCHE

Better not take a dog on the space shuttle because when he sticks his head out the window when you're coming home, his face might burn up. ■ *SATURDAY NIGHT LIVE*

My dogs sit up and look out the whole time and notice things, such as game getting up or other dogs on the roadside. One little cocker sings during the whole journey. ■ E. DOUGLAS WOLFF

An Airedale, erect beside the chauffeur of a Rolls-Royce,
Often gives you the impression he's there from choice.
■ E.B. WHITE

Berlinische Galerie, Bildarchiv Preussischer Kulturbesitz, Berlin

MONDO CANINE

PERMISSIONS/ ACKNOWLEDGMENTS

Excerpts from *We Think the World of You* by J.R. Ackerley, copyright (c) 1960 by J.R. Ackerley. Copyright (c) renewed 1988 by Francis King. Reprinted by permission of Poseidon Press, a division of Simon & Schuster, Inc.

"Adventure Dog" by Dave Barry, copyright (c) 1988 by Dave Barry. Reprinted by permission of Crown Publishers, Inc.

"The Most Beautiful Girl in the World" by Stanley Bing, copyright (c) 1989 by Stanley Bing. Reprinted by permission of the author. Originally in *Esquire*.

Excerpts from *A Celebration of Dogs*, copyright (c) 1982, 1984 by Rogar Caras. Reprinted by permission of the author.

"The Dog Who Paid Cash" from *Autobiography of Will Rogers* edited by Donald Day, copyright (c) 1949 by Rogers Co. Copyright (c) renewed 1977 by Donald Day and Beth Day. Reprinted by permission of Houghton Mifflin Company.

Ahbhu by Harlan Ellison is an extract from the story "The Deathbird" originally published in the author's collection, DEATHBIRD STORIES; copyright (c) 1973 by Harlan Ellison. Reprinted with permission of, and by arrangement with, the author and the author's agent, Richard Curtis Associates, Inc., New York. All rights reserved.

Excerpts from *Superdog: Raising the Perfect Canine Companion* by Dr. Michael W. Fox, copyright (c) 1990 by Michael W. Fox. Reprinted by permission of Howell House Books, an imprint of Macmillan Publishing Company.

Excerpts from *How to Talk to Your Animals* by Jean Craighead George, copyright (c) 1985 by Jean Craighead George. Reprinted by permission of Harcourt Brace Jovanovich, Inc.

Excerpts from *Adam's Task: Calling Animals by Name* by Vicki Hearne, copyright (c) 1982, 1983, 1985, 1986 by Vicki Hearne. Reprinted by permission of Alfred A. Knopf, Inc.

"Dogs That Have Known Me" from *Please Don't Eat the Daisies* by Jean Kerr, copyright (c) 1957 by Jean Kerr. Reprinted by permission of Doubleday, a division of Bantam Doubleday Dell Publishing Group, Inc.

INDEX OF HUMANS

259

261

INDEX OF DOGS

263

ABOUT THE AUTHOR

Jon Winokur is the editor/compiler of several books, including *The Portable Curmudgeon*, *Zen to Go*, and *Friendly Advice*. He lives in Pacific Palisades, California.